VIBRANT
FOOD

VIBRANT
FOOD

CELEBRATING the INGREDIENTS,
RECIPES, and COLORS of EACH SEASON

—

Written and Photographed by
KIMBERLEY HASSELBRINK

—

TEN SPEED PRESS
Berkeley

CONTENTS

INTRODUCTION

It was a head of overripe purple cauliflower—the last from my friend Nicole's winter garden—that began my obsession with colorful produce. The cauliflower was close to flowering, and probably a little bitter, but I was enamored. I had never seen purple cauliflower before or, at least, it had never captured my attention so completely. I began to consider vegetables differently—regarding them not in terms of what ingredients would make a meal but what colors inspired me. And once I began hunting for color, it popped up everywhere: the shocking fluorescent pink in the rib of a humble chard stem, the flecks of deep reds and purples in baby kale leaves, the pale shades of new green that emerged in the spring, and even the quiet yellows and whites in so many winter vegetables.

Thinking about produce in terms of color reinvigorated my relationship not only with food but also with photography. It brought me to a place of curiosity, an inquisitive examination of the natural world through its structure, its tones, and its hues. Formalizing this preoccupation with a new series on my blog, *The Year in Food*, was an easy next step. Called "Color Studies," the purpose of the series was to celebrate color in produce. The project resonated with people. And it captured and held my attention and interest. Hiding out in the Color Studies were the beginnings of this book.

One of the greatest discoveries in working on this book was that flavor and texture are equally important in creating a dish one can rightfully call vibrant.

I love to improvise in the kitchen, driven by a desire to experiment, to think about ingredients creatively, to brainstorm. *Vibrant Food* is the result of that brainstorming: its purpose is to start with color, employing flavor and texture to build gorgeous, dynamic dishes. My hope is that it is equal parts inspiration and accessibility. Even if you can't find nettles, fresh chickpeas, kumquats, quince, or some of the other less common ingredients I've grown so fond of, I hope that curiosity will get the better of you. Perhaps you'll bring a striking vegetable home and mull over it, and then build a colorful dish around that vegetable. That is how I cook.

Which is to say, this book showcases how I like to eat. Some colorful ingredient will capture my fancy, and I'll begin to think about it. I'll think about its texture, what would taste good with it, whether it needs sweet or salt or acid, and I'll build a recipe from there. We all have our preferences and quirks, and I don't think that mine have ever been more abundantly clear than in the process of making this book. If I had my way, I would add olive oil, Greek yogurt, feta cheese, chipotle powder, paprika, arugula, kale, cardamom, or eggs to nearly everything that I eat. They are the ingredients that I return to again and again.

And speaking of food preferences, one thing should be noted: I stopped eating wheat in November 2011. I did so because of long-term, chronic digestive issues that were deeply interfering with my ability to function and enjoy life. I had known for a long time that I should cut wheat out of my diet, but it was no easy task. When I finally did so, my digestion began to function healthily again, and I have kept with a gluten-free diet ever since. Most of the dishes in this book that use pasta noodles or wheat flour have been tested both with and without wheat gluten. I have grown to love how dynamic nut and grain flours are, and how much flavor and texture they add to a dish. The choice is yours to make. If you're partial to wheat noodles and wheat flour, carry on as you know. If you're curious about eating gluten-free, this is an opportunity to experiment with brown rice noodles, oat flour, almond flour, and the like.

SEASONALITY AND STRUCTURE

I love eating produce at the peak of its season. It's a very intuitive way of getting the best fruits and vegetables, and it's also an intuitive way to organize this book. But what's in season and when that season begins and ends is wildly variable depending on climate and location. So take it with a grain of salt. Some produce peaks late in its season, some produce straddles the end of one season and the beginning of another. I have organized the produce in each section according to when it peaks in the season, from early to late.

EATING INTUITIVELY

Sometimes the joy of food can get lost in the nuances of nutrition. Over the past few years, a lot of information has come out on the nutritive value of phytonutrients in colorful vegetables and fruits. I care deeply about what I eat, but not to the point that I will choose one vegetable over another because one has more antioxidants. And so goes this book: if we intuitively let color guide our choices, we can trust that we're eating well, and taking care of ourselves, and celebrating food for its dynamism, its vibrancy, its flavor, and its colors, as much as we are for its benefits to our health.

SPRING

The SOFT COLORS *of* SPRING

SPRING'S color palette is my favorite. It's all softness and pastel and light. What dominates spring produce is a range of magnificently tender green hues— the bright new growth of the season. Those soft greens are like the vegetable equivalent of a baby animal—they're gentle and welcoming. And then there are those wisps of pale lavender or soft pink streaking through the greens, and these are everywhere, too: in baby artichokes, spring onions, ramps, asparagus.

Spring is marked mostly by tender shoots and roots. Aside from late-winter citrus or the first apricots or berries that pass through quietly before the great storm of produce that ushers us gladly into summer, there's hardly any season-specific fruit around. Except rhubarb, which isn't truly a fruit but deserves its proud place in the pantheon of creative spring desserts—and defies my glorification of the soft and the bright of spring. Every season has its outlier.

Spring
GREENS

SPRING PEA *and*
PEA SHOOT OMELET

An omelet is a beautiful way to make use of those last little bits—a handful of fresh herbs or that lonely radish in the fridge—and elevate your breakfast to something fancy with minimal effort. This omelet sings springtime; between the soft goat cheese, fresh young peas, and delicate pea shoot tendrils, it's an homage to the greenest of seasons. Pea shoots are often found at the farmers' market in spring. Their flavor is like a muted, leafy version of a pea. You can easily scale this recipe up.

1 teaspoon unsalted butter

2 large eggs, whisked

Fine sea salt and freshly ground black pepper

¼ cup pea shoots, plus more for garnish

1 rounded tablespoon fresh shelled peas, plus more for garnish

1 tablespoon soft, fresh goat cheese, crumbled

1 teaspoon finely chopped fresh chives, plus more for garnish

½ teaspoon fresh whole thyme leaves

Heat an 8-inch skillet over low heat. Add the butter and melt. When the butter is bubbly, add the eggs, along with salt and pepper to taste. Using a heatproof rubber spatula, push the outer edge of the eggs toward the center of the pan, then tilt the skillet to distribute the eggs. Continue this way until the eggs have nearly set, which should only take a couple of minutes.

Add the pea shoots, peas, goat cheese, chives, and thyme to the center of the eggs. Turn off the heat, cover with a lid, and leave for 2 minutes.

To serve, fold half of the omelet over the filling and slide onto a plate. Garnish with pea shoots, peas, and chives.

MAKES 1 OMELET

FRESH CHICKPEAS
on TOAST

Fresh chickpeas—who knew? I discovered these last spring at the farmers' market. Eaten raw, they're crunchy and green, similar to a fresh pea. Cooking fresh chickpeas causes them to lose their soft green color and turn into the beige legume we all know. It was my friend Stacy's idea to pair these with toast—genius. They're a nod to the spring classic, peas on toast, but the chickpea flavor is a little quieter. Their shelling requires patience; listen to music and share the task with a handful of friends and a bottle of wine.

1 baguette, sliced into ½-inch rounds

3 tablespoons extra-virgin olive oil, plus more for brushing

16 ounces fresh chickpeas in their pods (about 2 cups shelled)

Zest and juice of 1 lemon

1 clove garlic, minced

2 tablespoons fresh mint cut into ribbons (chiffonade), plus more for serving

1 tablespoon coarsely chopped fresh dill, plus more for serving

¾ teaspoon fine sea salt

Freshly ground black pepper

1 cup ricotta

Preheat the oven to 350°F.

Place the bread slices on a baking sheet and brush each side lightly with olive oil. Toast the bread for about 20 minutes, turning once, until golden brown.

Meanwhile, prepare the chickpeas. Shell them and place in a medium bowl. You should have about 2 cups.

In a small bowl, whisk together the 3 tablespoons olive oil, lemon juice, garlic, mint, dill, ½ teaspoon of the salt, and pepper to taste. Pour the dressing over the chickpeas and toss to evenly distribute. Set aside.

In another bowl, combine the ricotta, lemon zest, and the remaining ¼ teaspoon salt.

Assemble the toasts by spreading about 2 teaspoons of the ricotta mixture over each toast, followed by a spoonful of chickpeas and a drizzle of their dressing. Garnish with mint, dill, and freshly ground pepper. Serve immediately.

SERVES 6 TO 8

WHOLE FAVA BEANS *with* LEMON *and* SHALLOTS

1 small shallot, thinly sliced

1 tablespoon red wine vinegar

¼ teaspoon fine sea salt

16 ounces small, tender fava beans in pods

3 tablespoons extra-virgin olive oil

¼ teaspoon dried red pepper flakes (optional)

2 to 3 thin lemon slices, quartered

Flaky sea salt, such as Maldon

Freshly ground black pepper

I first had whole, unshelled fava beans at a restaurant near my house, Slow Club, and it was a revelation. Pan-frying or grilling them whole not only eliminates the drudgery of shelling but also diminishes waste. Plus, they're a delight for guests—people won't expect them to be prepared this way and are almost always pleasantly surprised by their wonderfully charred flavor. Be sure to use tender, young fava beans whose pods are soft—older beans aren't enjoyable eaten in the pod, and you'll resent me for suggesting that you try them this way.

In a small mixing bowl, toss the shallots with the red wine vinegar and ¼ teaspoon salt. Set aside to marinate, tossing occasionally.

Heat a large skillet over medium heat. Add 1 tablespoon of the olive oil. Add about half of the fava beans in a single layer—you will likely have to work in batches. Fry without disturbing until their skin begins to blister and char in spots, 4 to 6 minutes. Flip the fava beans and repeat for another 2 to 3 minutes, removing them as they char. The pods will pop as steam builds inside—a few pods may burst, so be careful. Remove the first batch of pods and place on a wide, shallow serving dish. Repeat with the remaining fava beans.

Finish the dressing by adding the remaining 2 tablespoons of olive oil and the red pepper flakes to the shallot marinade.

Carefully toss the beans with the dressing and the lemon slices. Finish with a generous sprinkle of Maldon salt and freshly ground black pepper.

SERVES 4

PASTA *with* NETTLE PESTO *and* BLISTERED SNAP PEAS

One summer when we were kids, my sister leaped from the back patio of our cousins' home and into a large patch of stinging nettles. I remember everyone shouting when she was already midair, "Stephy, no!" but it was too late. The memory has always served as a great reminder for me to wear gloves when handling nettles. Once blanched, nettles lose their sting and take on a mild flavor, rather like a robust, faintly nutty spinach. And they grow everywhere—they're essentially a weed, making it easy to prepare this pesto with only some nuts and olive oil from the cupboard and a mess of nettles plucked from the backyard or a nearby park. To make this pasta gluten-free, try brown rice spaghetti noodles, which are my favorite.

Bring a large pot of salted water to a boil. Add the pasta and cook according to the package instructions, being sure to keep the pasta al dente. Reserve ½ cup of pasta water for the sauce and drain the pasta.

To make the pesto, bring a smaller pot of salted water to a boil. Blanch the nettles for about 30 seconds. Remove and submerge in an ice water bath for about 1 minute. Drain thoroughly and lightly squeeze out any excess water.

Combine the nettles, almonds, olive oil, Parmesan, garlic, and salt in a food processor. Pulse until smooth. If the pesto is thick, add some of the reserved pasta water. Set aside.

Heat a large skillet over a medium-high heat. Add the olive oil. Add the peas and sauté for 2 to 3 minutes without disturbing, until the shells have turned bright green and are blackened in spots. Flip the pods and cook for another 2 to 3 minutes.

Carefully toss the pasta with the nettle pesto and the peas. Top with crumbled feta. Serve hot.

SERVES 4 TO 6

12 ounces spaghetti

1 tablespoon extra-virgin olive oil

12 ounces sugar snap peas, ends and strings removed

1 cup crumbled feta cheese

NETTLE PESTO

5 cups firmly packed fresh nettles, rinsed

⅓ cup chopped raw almonds

¼ cup extra-virgin olive oil

¼ cup freshly grated Parmesan cheese

2 cloves garlic, minced

¼ teaspoon fine sea salt

ALLIUMS

BAKED EGGS *with* POLENTA *and* RAMPS

As a kid, I was fascinated by my mother's Foxfire collection, a series of books documenting life in rural Appalachian Georgia in the 1970s. One of the most celebrated spring rituals was the gathering of ramps, a wild leek abundant in the mountainous South—and once very much the food of the rural poor. Now their popularity has made them both more readily available and often quite expensive. But they're worth it as a weekend treat. Their unique flavor, reminiscent of garlic and leeks, is a perfect match with breakfast eggs, polenta, and fresh thyme. If you can't find ramps, try leeks or spring onions instead.

3⅓ cups low-sodium vegetable broth

⅔ cup coarse cornmeal

8 ounces ramps, thoroughly cleaned

⅓ cup grated Asiago cheese

1 teaspoon finely chopped fresh thyme

¾ teaspoon fine sea salt

Freshly ground black pepper

1 tablespoon unsalted butter

4 eggs

Bring the broth to a boil in a pot, then reduce the heat to low. Add the cornmeal in a slow, steady stream while stirring. Continue stirring regularly as the thick cornmeal cooks. The polenta will be ready in about 35 minutes, when the liquid is absorbed and the polenta pulls away from the side of the pot.

Meanwhile, preheat the oven to 400°F. Place four 8-ounce ramekins on a baking sheet and place the sheet in the cold oven to preheat while the polenta cooks.

Next, dice the white and pink ends of the ramps, keeping them separate from the leafy stalks. Coarsely chop the green ends.

When the polenta is cooked, remove from the heat. Stir in the Asiago cheese, thyme, ½ teaspoon of the salt, and freshly ground black pepper to taste. Set aside.

Heat a large skillet over medium-low heat. Add butter and melt. Add the white and pink ramp ends, stirring often. After about 2 minutes, add the greens. Stir until the greens are soft and wilted, another 2 to 3 minutes more. Add the remaining ¼ teaspoon salt, stir, and remove from the heat. Remove the ramekins from the oven. Grease them generously with butter, being careful not to burn yourself. Spoon about ⅓ cup of polenta into each (you will have some left over—tuck it into a lunch with some roasted vegetables), followed by a quarter of the ramps. Return the ramekins to the oven for 5 minutes.

Remove the ramekins from the oven and crack 1 egg into each. Bake for about 10 minutes, until the whites have set. Set aside to cool for 5 minutes, then serve.

SERVES 4

ROAST CHICKEN
with SPRING ONIONS
and SALSA VERDE

I love roast chicken for its reliability. It's straightforward to prepare, and dark meat is especially juicy and flavorful. Gorgeous purple and green spring onions turn soft and caramelized when nestled in the roasting pan, and a generous helping of Italian salsa verde adds a welcome burst of bright, green flavor to finish.

Preheat the oven to 425°F.

Rinse and dry the chicken legs with a paper towel, then generously sprinkle with salt and pepper. Set aside. Toss the spring onions with a little olive oil, salt, and pepper. Grease a 9 by 12-inch baking dish and arrange the chicken legs and spring onions in a single layer.

Roast for 25 to 30 minutes, until the thickest part of the leg registers 165°F on an instant-read thermometer. Let the meat rest for about 10 minutes.

While the meat is resting, prepare the salsa verde by whisking together the parsley, olive oil, capers, garlic, lemon zest, and salt in a small bowl.

Serve with salsa verde spooned over the chicken, and additional salsa on the side.

SERVES 4

4 whole chicken legs

Fine sea salt and freshly ground black pepper

6 small spring onions, stems and root end removed, halved lengthwise

Extra-virgin olive oil

SALSA VERDE

¾ cup finely chopped fresh flat-leaf parsley

¼ cup extra-virgin olive oil

1 tablespoon chopped capers

1 tablespoon minced garlic

Zest of 1 lemon

¼ teaspoon fine sea salt

Spring
ROOTS

ROASTED POTATO SALAD *with* ASPARAGUS *and a* BOILED EGG

7 tablespoons extra-virgin olive oil

½ cup finely chopped fresh basil

½ cup finely chopped fresh flat-leaf parsley

¼ cup freshly grated Parmesan cheese

3 tablespoons finely chopped fresh tarragon

2 cloves garlic, minced

¼ teaspoon fine sea salt, plus more to taste

2 pounds new potatoes, such as fingerling or yellow Finn, halved lengthwise

½ pound asparagus, sliced diagonally into ½-inch pieces

4 eggs, room temperature

2 to 3 radishes, sliced paper-thin

Chive blossoms or chives, for garnish

A handful of colorful vegetables and herbs are given heft with a pile of crispy new potatoes and a medium-boiled egg. The mellowed onion flavor of lavender-hued chive blossoms stands in for green chives in this celebration of spring, but feel free to use regular chives if you can't get your hands on their blossoms. Softer-skinned, sweeter new potatoes make their debut in the springtime—look for them at your local farmers' market.

Preheat the oven to 400°F.

To prepare the herb sauce, combine 4 tablespoons of the olive oil with the basil, parsley, Parmesan, tarragon, garlic, and ¼ teaspoon salt. Set aside.

Toss the potatoes in 2 tablespoons of the olive oil. Arrange them in a single layer cut side up on a baking sheet. Sprinkle with sea salt. Roast for about 25 to 30 minutes, turning them once, until fork tender but firm.

Meanwhile, prepare the eggs. Bring a medium pot of water to a gentle boil. Using a slotted spoon, carefully place the eggs in the gently simmering water. Cook for 7 minutes, or longer for a firmer yolk. Remove the eggs with the spoon and place in an ice water bath for about 3 minutes. Gently remove the shell from each egg and slice in half lengthwise.

Warm a large skillet over medium heat. Add the remaining tablespoon of olive oil and the asparagus. Sauté the asparagus for 4 minutes, stirring occasionally. Set aside.

Combine the warm potatoes with the herb sauce. Add the asparagus and gently mix. Divide among four plates, placing one egg on each plate. Finish with a few radish slices and a sprinkle of chive blossoms. Serve warm.

SERVES 4

EDAMAME *and* RADISH RISOTTO

I sometimes find the bracing flavor of a radish slightly overpowering. Quickly sautéing them in a little butter changes their character completely. And as long as you keep the cooking time short, they'll retain their bright colors. Here, edamame riffs on the more traditional role of spring peas in risotto.

Heat the broth in a small pot over the lowest heat setting. Keep warm, but do not allow it to simmer.

In a large skillet or stockpot over medium-low heat, melt 1 tablespoon of the butter. Add the onion and sauté until translucent, about 5 minutes. Add the garlic and sauté for 1 minute more, stirring frequently to keep garlic from burning. Add the rice and sauté until toasted, 5 minutes, stirring regularly.

Add ½ cup of the broth and stir regularly. When the rice has absorbed most of the broth, add another ½ cup. Continue adding broth until most of it has been absorbed. When the rice is done, it will be creamy but firm. Add the edamame and stir for 1 minute more. Turn off the heat. Stir in the Parmesan, thyme, ½ teaspoon of the salt, and pepper to taste.

Warm a skillet over medium-low heat. Add the remaining 1 tablespoon butter. When the butter is melted, add the radish halves, white sides down, and sauté until the radishes have softened but retain their color, 3 to 4 minutes. Sprinkle with the remaining ¼ teaspoon salt and toss gently.

Divide the risotto among four bowls and top with the radishes. Serve warm.

SERVES 4

4½ cups low-sodium vegetable broth

2 tablespoons unsalted butter

1 small yellow onion, diced

2 cloves garlic, minced

1 cup Arborio rice

1¼ cups shelled edamame

½ cup freshly grated Parmesan cheese

1 teaspoon minced fresh thyme

¾ teaspoon fine sea salt

Freshly ground black pepper

1 bunch radishes (about 15) halved lengthwise

ROASTED SARDINES *with* CARROT FENNEL SLAW

Sardines are one of those underappreciated species of fish that deserve more accolades than they receive. In California, they're abundant and cheap. Plus, they're healthy and a cinch to prepare. Fresh sardines are nothing like their tinned cousins; their flavor is rich and far more delicate. Dressed with a miso glaze and augmented by gorgeous strands of rainbow carrot and a little fresh fennel crunch, this is a wonderful, light spring meal.

Preheat the oven to 400°F.

To prepare the slaw, whisk together the brown rice vinegar, sugar, salt, and red pepper flakes. Thoroughly rinse the outer skin of the carrots. Use a vegetable peeler to peel the carrots along their length, creating long ribbons. Place in a mixing bowl. Next, slice the fennel crosswise very thinly with a sharp knife or mandoline. Reserve the fennel fronds for garnish. Toss the brown rice vinegar mix with the carrots and fennel. Set aside.

If your sardines have not been gutted by your fishmonger, do this now. Slice each sardine along the length of the belly and remove the organs by gently pulling them out with your fingers. Rinse thoroughly under cool water. Drain on paper towels and blot dry.

Combine the miso, mirin, brown rice vinegar, brown sugar, and garlic with a fork to make a paste. Arrange the fish on a baking sheet. Brush the insides of the sardines with the miso paste. Brush the outsides of the fish with the sesame oil.

Roast the sardines until cooked through, about 8 minutes.

Using tongs, remove the slaw from the bowl, draining off any excess liquid, and divide between four plates. Top each with two sardines and finish with a few fennel fronds.

SERVES 4

CARROT FENNEL SLAW

¼ cup brown rice vinegar

1 teaspoon natural cane sugar

¼ teaspoon fine sea salt

¼ teaspoon dried red pepper flakes

6 rainbow carrots

1 small fennel bulb with fronds, cored

8 large sardines

3 tablespoons white miso

1 tablespoon mirin

1 tablespoon brown rice vinegar

1 teaspoon brown sugar

1 clove garlic, minced

Toasted sesame oil

RHUBARB

RHUBARB COMPOTE
with CACAO NIBS

16 ounces rhubarb, trimmed
and cut into 1-inch pieces

½ cup honey

¼ cup water

Juice of 1 lemon

1 vanilla bean, split lengthwise

Crème fraîche, for serving

Cacao nibs, for serving

Rhubarb's bracing, tart flavors come alive in this dessert. I love the crunch and savory chocolate notes that the cacao nibs provide, along with the cool tang of crème fraîche. It's an intoxicating mix.

In a large pot, combine the rhubarb, honey, water, and lemon juice. Scrape the seeds from the vanilla bean into the pot, and toss the pod in as well. Stir gently to combine. Bring the mixture to a boil. Reduce to a simmer and cook, covered, for 12 to 15 minutes, stirring halfway.

Remove from the heat and allow to cool slightly. Discard the vanilla bean pod. Divide the compote among 4 bowls. Serve warm or at room temperature with a dollop of crème fraîche and a generous sprinkling of cacao nibs.

SERVES 4

RHUBARB GINGER FIZZ

Rhubarb's dramatic pink color is given pride of place in this striking cocktail. Ginger and lime make it perfectly refreshing. The syrup that is made here could be put to good use on its own with sparkling water.

To make the syrup, combine the rhubarb, ginger, water, and sugar in a pot. Bring to a boil, then reduce the heat and simmer, covered, until the rhubarb has fallen apart, 12 to 15 minutes. Remove from the heat and set aside to cool.

Strain the mixture through a fine sieve or cheesecloth, using the back of a large wooden spoon to extract as much liquid as possible. Strain a second time if you prefer a very clear syrup. You should have about 14 ounces (just shy of 2 cups) of liquid. Chill in the fridge until cold, at least 2 hours.

Slice 1 lime into thin rounds and set aside. For each drink, in a cocktail shaker, combine 3 ounces (6 tablespoons) of the rhubarb syrup, 1½ ounces (3 tablespoons) gin, 1½ ounces (3 tablespoons) sparkling water, the juice of ½ lime, and a few ice cubes. Stir well, then strain into a chilled coupe glass and garnish with a thin slice of lime. Repeat to make four servings.

SERVES 4

RHUBARB SYRUP

16 ounces rhubarb, sliced into ¼-inch to ½-inch pieces

2 ounces fresh ginger, chopped

1½ cups water

¾ cup natural cane sugar

3 limes

6 ounces (¾ cup) gin

6 ounces (¾ cup) seltzer water

Ice, for serving

FLOWERS

VIBRANT FOOD

NASTURTIUM SALAD

¼ cup sunflower seeds

4 cups firmly packed nasturtium leaves

2 small pluots, pitted and thinly sliced lengthwise

¼ cup crumbled blue cheese

Petals from 4 to 5 nasturtium flowers

CHAMPAGNE VINAIGRETTE

1½ teaspoons Champagne vinegar

1½ teaspoons minced shallot

1½ teaspoons honey

1½ tablespoons extra-virgin olive oil

Fine sea salt and freshly ground black pepper

This is the salad for the frustrated gardener whose plants are being choked to death by aggressive nasturtium vines. Instead of tossing out the vines, you can incorporate the leaves and flowers into a salad. The leaves have the same peppery flavor as the flowers, but without the sweetness. And that pepperiness is tamed a little by dressing them. Nasturtiums have a long growing season along California's mild coast, but pluots and nasturtiums are only in season together for a brief window in late spring and early summer. If you can't find pluots, use their parent fruits—apricots and plums—instead. And if you don't have a backyard full of nasturtiums, try using watercress or arugula. *See photo, page 41.*

To toast the sunflower seeds, heat a dry skillet over medium-low heat. Add the sunflower seeds and stir frequently until golden brown, 3 to 4 minutes. Set aside to cool.

To make the vinaigrette, in a small mixing bowl, whisk together the Champagne vinegar, shallot, honey, and olive oil. Season to taste with salt and pepper.

Toss the nasturtium leaves with the vinaigrette. Divide the leaves among four plates and top the leaves with one-quarter each of the sunflower seeds, pluot slices, blue cheese, and nasturtium petals. Serve immediately.

SERVES 4

SQUASH BLOSSOM *and* GREEN CORIANDER QUESADILLAS.

These quesadillas only have five ingredients. And while the squash blossoms and fresh coriander seeds may be a little tricky to find outside a farmers' market or your own garden, they're worth hunting down. A squash blossom's flavor is quiet—like all edible flowers, it tastes like a softer version of its vegetal offspring. Each bite of the quesadilla offers something different: a delicate, faint zucchini flavor, a pop of bright green coriander seeds, or a note of heat from the pepper Jack. If you grow zucchini or any variety of summer squash, you can pluck the male flowers from the vine and save on the cost of squash blossoms, which are sometimes pricy at the grocery. They're usually less expensive at a farmers' market. Look for fresh blossoms that haven't wilted. Substitute coarsely chopped fresh cilantro leaves if you can't find fresh coriander. *See photo, page 45.*

12 squash blossoms

6 corn tortillas

1½ cups coarsely shredded pepper Jack cheese

1 tablespoon fresh, green coriander seeds

Freshly ground black pepper

Look over the squash blossoms and brush off any dirt or small bugs you might find. The blossoms are very delicate, so do not wash them. Some people remove the stamens, but it isn't necessary.

Warm a cast-iron skillet or other heavy pan over medium heat. Place a tortilla in the warm pan and heat each side for about 15 seconds to soften. Sprinkle about ¼ cup of the cheese, ½ teaspoon coriander seeds, and pepper on half of the tortilla. Place two squash blossoms on top of the cheese, with the flower petals at the edge of the tortilla so that they peek out slightly. Fold the tortilla in half and press down lightly with a spatula. Cook for about 1 minute, then flip and cook the other side for 1 minute more, until the tortilla is thoroughly warmed and the cheese has melted. Transfer to a paper towel-lined plate and make five more quesadillas. Serve warm.

MAKES 6 QUESADILLAS

VIBRANT FOOD

CHOCOLATE TRUFFLES
with BEE POLLEN

⅓ cup heavy whipping cream

3 ounces high-quality bittersweet chocolate (at least 65% cacao)

2 to 3 tablespoons bee pollen

I first became familiar with bee pollen for its supposed allergy benefits. There was a jar of it sitting neglected in my fridge for months—until I dipped a spoon in, tried a little, and was hooked. The flavor is heavenly—a sweet-tart citrus taste with an intoxicating floral note. It's an amazing partner with a strong, dark chocolate. Please note that if you're allergic to honey, you shouldn't eat bee pollen either.

To make the ganache, in a small saucepan, bring the heavy whipping cream to a low simmer. While the cream heats, coarsely chop the chocolate and place in a mixing bowl.

When the cream begins to bubble, remove the pan from the heat and pour the liquid over the chocolate. Whisk the chocolate and cream together steadily until the chocolate is thoroughly melted and the mixture is smooth. Chill for at least 1 hour.

While the ganache is cooling, prepare the bee pollen. Using the flat side of a large knife or a mortar and pestle, press the bee pollen until it breaks down. The bee pollen should have a powdery, crumbled texture. Place this in a small bowl and set aside until you are ready to prepare the truffles.

To make the truffles, measure 1 scant teaspoon of ganache and use your fingers to form it into a rough ball (like a small pebble). Roll the truffle in the bee pollen to thoroughly coat. Repeat with the remaining ganache. Store the truffles in a tightly sealed container and keep in the fridge for no more than 3 days. The truffles have a tendency to melt a little in the fingers at room temperature, so serve them chilled, straight from the fridge.

MAKES 24 TO 28 TRUFFLES

CHOCOLATE POTS DE CRÈME *with* LAVENDER *and* SEA SALT

CHOCOLATE POTS DE CRÈME

2 cups whole milk or plain almond milk

¼ cup natural cane sugar

¼ teaspoon fine sea salt

½ vanilla bean, split

4 ounces bittersweet chocolate (at least 65% cacao), coarsely chopped

1 large egg plus 3 large yolks

SUGARED FLOWERS

¼ cup natural cane sugar

12 to 18 edible small culinary lavender blooms, borage flowers, and/or violets

1 large egg white

Flaky sea salt, such as Maldon

This dessert was inspired by a chocolate lavender bar made by Dagoba, one of my favorite brands. I love the way the essence of the flower quietly permeates the chocolate. While these pots de crème have gone in a very different direction, they still hold on to that essence. This is definitely a fancy dessert for a special occasion when you have the time for making both the pots de crème and the candied flowers. It's important to use culinary lavender for this recipe, ideally *Lavandula angustifolia* (English lavender), and to seek out young buds. Older buds will yield a bitter flavor. You can make these with almond milk or regular milk. If using almond milk, be sure to find one with a higher fat content, and absolutely no sweetener or flavoring. *See photo, page 49.*

In a saucepan over medium-low heat, combine the milk, sugar, and salt. Scrape the seeds from the vanilla bean and add to the saucepan along with the pod. Heat until the milk is hot and steaming, stirring to dissolve the sugar; do not let the milk boil. Remove the pan from the heat.

Preheat the oven to 325°F. Place six 4- to 6-ounce custard cups or jars in a roasting pan. Have plenty of boiling water ready.

Put the chocolate in a heatproof bowl. Strain the milk mixture through a fine-mesh sieve over the chocolate, stirring gently until the chocolate is melted and smooth, about 1 to 2 minutes. Rinse the saucepan and scrape the chocolate mixture back into the pan. Warm gently over medium-low heat until hot and steaming, stirring occasionally.

Add the egg and yolks to the heatproof bowl and whisk together until combined. Slowly pour the chocolate mixture over the eggs, whisking constantly, until combined. Strain the mixture through a fine-mesh sieve into a measuring pitcher; you should have about 3 cups. Divide the mixture among the custard cups and skim any bubbles from the top of each. Place the roasting pan in the oven and add boiling water to the roasting pan to come approximately halfway up the sides of the cups. Bake until the custards are nearly set and jiggle slightly in the center, 25 to 30 minutes.

Remove the pan from the oven. Transfer the cups to a wire rack to cool completely, about 1 hour. Cover each custard cup with plastic wrap and refrigerate until well chilled, about 4 hours.

While the custards are chilling, make the sugared flowers. Reduce the oven heat to 170°F. Line a rimmed baking sheet with parchment paper. Place the sugar in a small bowl. Using a small paintbrush and holding the bloom on the bud end, coat each flower with a very thin layer of egg white. Dip the flower into the sugar, shake off the excess, and lay on the sheet pan with the stem end down. Repeat with the remaining flowers. Place in the oven until the flowers are dried to the touch, about 1½ hours. Set aside to cool completely.

To serve, top each pot de crème with some of the sugared flowers and a sprinkle of flaky salt.

SERVES 6

SUMMER

The BOLD COLORS *of* SUMMER

SUMMER is the reward for the rest of the year. I do my best to make the most of winter produce, to appreciate all of its nuance and understated delight, but it is no match for summer's riotous glory. Summer's produce comes in big and loud and fun and full of boisterous color. It is the season of not holding back: those snazzy reds and bright yellows and bold oranges and deep purples and big, rich greens. It is the season forever tied to leisure and joy and simplicity. This comes through in the cooking, too—it is the easiest time of year to let fruits and vegetables be the stars with a minimum of fuss. We can dine outdoors and present a big plate of tomatoes drizzled with olive oil and fresh herbs as a fine thing all on its own. There is an urgency to it; so much is available, and so much of it is so briefly available. I want to eat every last tomato, every berry, all the melons, and the corn, and the peaches, and the cherries, until there is none left. Which is what I do, for a few months every year.

BERRIES

GRILLED HALLOUMI *with* STRAWBERRIES *and* HERBS

DRESSING

3 tablespoons extra-virgin olive oil

2 tablespoons freshly squeezed lime juice

2 teaspoons agave nectar

1 serrano chile, seeds removed if desired, minced

Freshly ground black pepper

6 ounces strawberries, hulled and sliced

1 tablespoon extra-virgin olive oil

1 (8- to 9-ounce) package halloumi cheese, cut into 8 slices

2 tablespoons chopped fresh mint

2 tablespoons chopped fresh cilantro

I was inspired to make this by some snacks brought to a picnicky party: my friend Dafna's spicy jalapeño jam and my friend Andy's halloumi cheese. We grilled the cheese and doused it with the jam and it was the undeniable hit of the party. I liked the idea of going for something spicy, sweet, and fresh on top of this intriguing cheese, so I made a mess of strawberries and herbs to pile atop it for this version. Halloumi is a firm, salty cheese that keeps its shape when grilled or fried in a pan. It's an awesome way to enjoy the unique pleasure of hot, melty cheese as a vehicle for food. It's best to eat the cheese as soon as possible after it's come out of the pan—the magic of halloumi happens when it's hot.

To make the dressing, whisk together the olive oil, lime juice, agave nectar, serrano, and pepper to taste. Toss the strawberries with the dressing and set aside.

Heat a very large skillet over medium-high heat and add the 1 tablespoon olive oil. When hot, add the halloumi slices. Cook the cheese for 2 to 3 minutes per side without disturbing, until a deep brown crust forms.

Remove the cheese from the skillet and spoon the strawberry mixture over the slices of cheese. Serve immediately, while the cheese is still warm.

SERVES 4 TO 6

ROSÉ SANGRIA

Swapping the more commonly found fruit in sangria, usually apples and oranges, for a mix of seasonal berries, like these lovely golden raspberries, along with some juicy watermelon, adds a welcome summery twist to this fresh, pink-hued drink. I prefer to use agave nectar with cold drinks because it blends more easily than honey, but if you have honey on hand, it's just fine as a substitute.

In a large pitcher, combine the rosé, Triple Sec, and agave nectar. Add the raspberries, watermelon, peach, and lime and gently stir to combine. Chill for 3 to 4 hours. Serve cold, over ice.

SERVES 4 TO 6

1 (750 ml) bottle crisp dry rosé

3 tablespoons Triple Sec or Grand Marnier

3 tablespoons agave nectar

1 cup raspberries, a mix of golden and red preferably

½ cup cubed watermelon

½ peach, thinly sliced

5 to 6 thin slices lime

Ice, for serving

SUMMER BERRY–COCONUT MILK ICE POPS

⅔ cup thinly sliced ripe strawberries

⅔ cup ripe blueberries

⅔ cup ripe blackberries

⅓ cup plus 1 tablespoon natural cane sugar

½ teaspoon ground cardamom

1 (13.5-ounce) can full-fat coconut milk

I love those instances when so few ingredients come together to make something so big in flavor and so deeply satisfying. The jammy mash-up of berries with the coconut milk and cardamom makes these pops just rich enough and rather irresistible. They never last long in the freezer.

Combine the strawberries, blueberries, and blackberries with the sugar and cardamom in a small saucepan. Cook over low heat, stirring regularly, for 5 to 7 minutes, until the berries are soft but not falling apart—they should be a little jammy. Remove from the heat and stir in the coconut milk. Carefully pour the warm berry mixture into a pitcher. Pour the mix into 3-ounce molds, helping some of the berries along with a spoon so that they're evenly distributed. Freeze for at least 4 hours. The ice pops will last a month in the freezer.

MAKES 10 (3-OUNCE) POPS

VIBRANT FOOD

Stone
FRUITS

CHERRY GINGER GRANOLA *with* PEACHES

3 cups old-fashioned rolled oats

1 cup raw almonds

½ cup raw pistachios

½ cup raw, shelled pumpkin seeds

1 cup unsweetened coconut flakes

1 teaspoon ground cinnamon

½ teaspoon ground ginger

¾ teaspoon fine sea salt

¾ cup maple syrup

¼ cup extra-virgin olive oil

1 teaspoon vanilla extract

¾ cup dried cherries

½ cup chopped crystallized ginger

Plain yogurt

2 peaches, thinly sliced lengthwise

I like to put lots of stuff in my granola—for variety, crunch, and flavor. The crystallized ginger perfumes the entire batch after it sits in a jar for a day, and the sweet-tart pucker of the dried cherries and the warmth of toasted coconut are lovely details. Any fresh summer fruit will make this an amazing bowl of goodness on a hurried (or leisurely) morning.

Preheat the oven to 300°F.

In a large mixing bowl, combine the oats, almonds, pistachios, pumpkin seeds, coconut flakes, cinnamon, ginger, and salt. In a small bowl, whisk together the maple syrup, olive oil, and vanilla. Pour over the dry ingredients and mix thoroughly to combine.

Spread the mixture evenly on a large, rimmed baking sheet. Bake for about 40 minutes, tossing every 10 minutes, until the granola is golden brown and well toasted.

Add the dried cherries and crystallized ginger and mix to combine. Set aside to cool. Store the granola in an airtight glass jar in a cool, dark place. It should keep for a week.

Serve with yogurt and about six peach slices per serving.

SERVES 4 TO 6

GREEN RICE SALAD *with* NECTARINES *and* CORN

This just might be the most refreshing salad I've ever eaten. Green rice is a great starting point for a big, summery grain salad. The sweetness of the corn and nectarine plays well off the cool, green herbal notes and the heat of the rice, rich with cilantro, jalapeño, and green onion. Cheese, as always, makes it even better.

In a saucepan, combine the rice and water, cover, and bring to a boil. Lower the heat and simmer, covered, until the liquid has been absorbed and the rice is tender, about 30 minutes. Let the rice stand for a few minutes, then fluff. Set aside to cool to room temperature.

Preheat the broiler.

To grill the corn, lightly oil both ears of corn and place in a small baking dish. Broil about 6 inches from the heat source, turning every few minutes, until golden and blackened in spots, 10 to 15 minutes. Transfer to a plate and set aside until cool enough to handle. Using a large, sharp knife, cut the kernels from the cob to yield about 1 cup. If you have more than this amount, save it for another use. Transfer the kernels to a bowl and toss with a pinch of salt and a squeeze of lime. Set aside.

Transfer the rice to a large bowl. In a blender, combine the cilantro, parsley, jalapeño, lime zest and juice, olive oil, a pinch of salt, and 1 tablespoon water. Blend until smooth. Add up to 1 more tablespoon of water to thin the sauce if it's too thick. Spoon the mixture over the rice, scraping any remaining sauce out of the blender with a spatula, and mix until the rice is evenly coated.

To finish, add the corn and additional parsley and cilantro to the rice. Toss to combine. Transfer the rice to a serving platter. Sprinkle the nectarines and queso fresco over the rice in even layers. Garnish with additional parsley and cilantro. Best served immediately. Can be made up to a day in advance; bring to room temperature before serving.

SERVES 4 TO 6

GREEN RICE

¾ cup brown basmati rice

1¼ cups water, plus 1 to 2 tablespoons more for sauce

½ cup coarsely chopped fresh cilantro

¼ cup loosely packed fresh flat-leaf parsley leaves

1 small jalapeño, seeded and chopped

Zest and juice of 1 small lime

1 tablespoon extra-virgin olive oil

Fine sea salt

GRILLED CORN

2 small ears fresh corn, husks and silk removed

Extra-virgin olive oil

Fine sea salt

½ lime

2 tablespoons fresh flat-leaf parsley leaves, plus more for garnish

¼ cup loosely packed fresh cilantro leaves, plus more for garnish

2 medium-ripe nectarines, pitted and thinly sliced lengthwise

½ cup crumbled queso fresco

APRICOT *and* CHICKEN SALAD *with* TOASTED CUMIN VINAIGRETTE

TOASTED CUMIN
VINAIGRETTE

1 tablespoon cumin seeds

2 tablespoons freshly squeezed lemon juice

2 tablespoons brown rice vinegar

1 teaspoon honey

¾ teaspoon sweet paprika

¼ teaspoon fine sea salt, plus more to taste

¼ cup extra-virgin olive oil

1½ tablespoons finely chopped fresh cilantro leaves

1 tablespoon finely chopped fresh flat-leaf parsley

Freshly ground black pepper

½ cup sliced raw almonds

2 cups shredded cooked chicken (about 10 ounces)

4 fresh apricots (about 8 ounces), pitted and sliced

6 cups loosely packed wild arugula

Apricots can be so fussy. At their peak, they are heavenly, marvelous fruit, but so often what's available at the supermarket is underripe and a little bland. Go for fragrant, rosy gold apricots at the peak of their season. The vibrant flavors of cumin and green herbs make this salad really sing. It's great as a hearty weekday lunch.

To make the vinaigrette, in a small frying pan over medium-low heat, toast the cumin seeds until golden and fragrant, about 3 minutes, stirring regularly. Grind the seeds in a spice grinder or mortar and pestle. In a bowl, whisk together the lemon juice, vinegar, honey, cumin, paprika, and salt. Gradually whisk in the oil until the vinaigrette is emulsified. Whisk in the cilantro and parsley. Season with pepper.

To make the salad, in the same small frying pan, toast the almonds over medium-low heat, stirring often, until golden and fragrant, about 4 minutes. Set aside to cool.

In a large serving bowl, toss together the chicken, apricots, half of the almonds, and the arugula. Drizzle with 3 to 4 tablespoons of the vinaigrette and toss gently until the vinaigrette is evenly distributed. Garnish with the remaining almonds and season to taste with more salt if desired. Serve with the remaining vinaigrette on the side. Store any leftover vinaigrette in an airtight container in the refrigerator for up to 3 days.

SERVES 4 TO 6

POACHED APRICOTS
with ROSE WATER

2 cups water

¼ cup honey

1 tablespoon rose water (not extract), such as Sadaf brand

¼ teaspoon ground cardamom

6 to 8 apricots (about 16 ounces), halved and pits removed

½ cup plain Greek yogurt, for serving (optional)

An apricot becomes a meltingly luxurious thing when poached—and those qualities are highlighted by the addition of fragrant rose water. Rose water is exactly what it sounds like: a simple infusion of rose petals in water. It's not as exotic or hard to find as you might think. Ask at your local supermarket— many carry it.

In a medium pot, bring the water and honey to a boil. Reduce the heat and add the rose water, cardamom, and apricot halves. Poach the apricots in the simmering liquid for 2 to 5 minutes, until the apricots are tender but hold their shape.

Turn off the heat and, using a slotted spoon, remove the apricots from the syrup and set aside. Bring the syrup to a boil over high heat and reduce by half, 15 to 20 minutes.

To serve, divide the apricot halves among six plates. Add a dollop of yogurt on top of each if desired, and drizzle the reduced rose water syrup over the apricots and yogurt.

SERVES 4 TO 6

CHERRY BUTTERMILK CLAFOUTIS

I love the word clafoutis—a charming name for a simple dessert. Without those sweet-tart cherries dominating every bite, it would be nothing more than a straightforward custard. But the cherries elevate it. And the buttermilk lends a welcome tang that gives it a little edge over using regular milk in a clafoutis. I like to use brown rice flour in place of all-purpose flour when I can, which I recommend here to make this dish gluten-free.

½ cup natural cane sugar

16 ounces sweet cherries, pitted

3 eggs

1¼ cups buttermilk

⅓ cup almond flour

2 tablespoons brown rice or all-purpose flour

2 teaspoons vanilla extract

2 teaspoons finely grated fresh ginger

¼ teaspoon fine sea salt

Confectioners' sugar, for dusting

Preheat the oven to 375°F. Grease a 9-inch pie pan with unsalted butter. Sprinkle with 1 tablespoon of the sugar.

Arrange the cherries in a single layer on the bottom of the pan. Set aside.

In a bowl, whisk together the eggs, buttermilk, remaining sugar, almond flour, brown rice flour, vanilla, ginger, and salt until smooth. Pour evenly over the fruit.

Bake for about 50 minutes, until golden brown around the edges and set in the center. Test by inserting a toothpick in the center—if it comes out clean, the clafoutis is ready.

Allow to cool slightly, then dust with confectioners' sugar and serve.

SERVES 6

SUMMER BERRY
and PEACH CRISP

FILLING

3 ripe yellow peaches, thinly sliced

1 cup blackberries

1 cup blueberries

1 cup hulled and quartered strawberries

⅓ cup natural cane sugar

2 tablespoons freshly squeezed lemon juice

1 tablespoon all-purpose flour

½ teaspoon ground ginger

TOPPING

2 cups old-fashioned rolled oats

1 cup coarsely chopped raw almonds

⅓ cup oat flour

⅓ cup lightly packed brown sugar

½ teaspoon salt

½ teaspoon ground cinnamon

½ teaspoon ground ginger

½ cup (1 stick) cold unsalted butter, cut into small cubes

Ice cream, for serving

Time and again, I've confirmed that a crisp packed with summer fruits is my all-time favorite dessert. It's the interplay of the sweet and the savory, the crunch of the topping with the luscious, falling-apart fruit, and the cool ice cream against the warm filling that makes this straightforward dessert so deeply satisfying. I like to let my ice cream melt a little—soupy ice cream was my favorite as a kid. I prefer a crisp with less sugar; if your fruit is on the less-ripe side, you may want to add a little more.

Preheat the oven to 375°F.

To make the filling, in a large mixing bowl, combine the peaches, blackberries, blueberries, and strawberries. Gently fold in the sugar, lemon juice, flour, and ginger. Pour the fruit filling into a shallow 2 to 2½-quart baking dish.

To prepare the topping, in another large bowl, combine the oats, almonds, oat flour, brown sugar, salt, cinnamon, and ginger. Add the butter and use your fingers to work the dry ingredients and butter together to form a loose mixture. Sprinkle evenly over the fruit.

Bake for 30 to 35 minutes, until the crisp is golden brown and bubbling at the edges. Allow to cool for 5 to 10 minutes. Serve warm, topped with ice cream.

SERVES 8 TO 10

Summer GREENS
and HERBS

THAI CHOPPED SALAD
with TOFU

This is a perfect catch-all for your summertime produce surplus. Use it as a template: make the tofu and the dressing, and add or subtract any type of sweet and crunchy vegetables you prefer. I happen to adore okra in all of its forms, but I realize that it's a polarizing vegetable. Try jicama or a sweet red pepper instead. And take advantage of summer's beautiful, bright salad greens: try Little Gem, a sturdy romaine, or baby oak leaf lettuce. Don't be shy with the herbs, either—this is a great place to feature gorgeous purple basil, heirloom mint varieties, or a smattering of flowering herb tops, such as those from basil, cilantro or mint, for a garnish. Look for Thai Kitchen brand for both the roasted red chili paste and the green curry paste.

To prepare the tofu, place the tofu on a plate and weight it with another heavy plate on top. Set aside to press for 30 minutes.

Meanwhile, to make the marinade, in a medium bowl, whisk together the tamari, brown rice vinegar, olive oil, red chili paste, and sugar until smooth. When the tofu is ready, dry it with a paper towel and cut into 1-inch cubes. Add to the bowl with the marinade and toss gently to coat. Cover, chill, and allow to marinate for at least 1 hour, or overnight.

Preheat the broiler. Arrange the tofu in a single layer on a lightly oiled, small baking sheet, discarding the marinade. Broil about 6 inches from the flame for 15 to 18 minutes, turning every 3 minutes or so, until deeply browned. Set aside.

While the tofu broils, make the dressing. Whisk together the lime juice and zest, fish sauce, brown sugar, and red pepper flakes until the brown sugar has dissolved.

To prepare the salad, combine the okra, beans, tomatoes, cucumbers, mint leaves, and basil. Toss with about two-thirds of the dressing, serving the remaining dressing on the side or reserving for another use. (Use it with any simple salad for bright flavor.) Serve atop a bed of lettuce, topped with the tofu and garnished with fresh cilantro leaves and flowers and sliced Thai red chile.

SERVES 4

1 (16-ounce) package extra-firm tofu, drained

¼ cup low-sodium tamari

2 tablespoons brown rice vinegar

2 tablespoons extra-virgin olive oil, plus additional oil for broiling

2 tablespoons roasted red chili paste

2 teaspoons natural cane sugar

2 heaping cups small okra, sliced into ½-inch rounds

2 cups sliced green or purple snap beans

2 cups halved cherry tomatoes

2 cups cubed cucumber

¼ cup loosely packed fresh mint leaves, plus more for garnish

¼ cup chopped fresh basil leaves, plus more for garnish

2 small heads Little Gem or butter lettuce, rinsed and torn

Cilantro leaves and blossoms, for garnish

1 small Thai red chile, seeded and thinly sliced, for garnish

LIME DRESSING
Juice of 2 limes, plus zest of 1 lime

3 tablespoons fish sauce

3 tablespoons brown sugar

¼ teaspoon red pepper flakes

SALMON BANH MI

PICKLED VEGETABLES

2 medium carrots

2 watermelon radishes (about 4 ounces total), or substitute daikon radish

⅓ English cucumber

½ cup distilled white vinegar

¼ cup natural cane sugar

½ teaspoon fine sea salt

AÏOLI

½ cup mayonnaise

1 small clove garlic, finely minced

Zest of ½ lemon

¼ cup boiling water

¼ cup lightly packed brown sugar

¼ cup fish sauce

1 tablespoon Sriracha chili sauce

1 teaspoon low-sodium tamari

3 cloves garlic, finely minced

16 ounces skinless wild salmon fillet (preferably thin), pinbones removed, cut into four equal pieces

1 French, Vietnamese, or gluten-free baguette, sliced crosswise into four equal pieces (about 5 to 6 inches long)

¼ cup loosely packed fresh cilantro leaves

¼ cup loosely packed fresh Thai basil leaves

1 small jalapeño, very thinly sliced (optional)

When I was a teenager, there was a particular sandwich from a nondescript corner store that I fell in love with. It cost all of two dollars, and it was amazing—full to bursting with all of these wild, bright, sweet and savory flavors. It wasn't until a few years ago that I realized that the cheap sandwich I bought in twos and threes to squirrel away in the fridge was a banh mi. There's nothing traditional about putting salmon in banh mi, but I had summer in mind with this iteration and seafood is a great fit. The Vietnamese baguette on which this is traditionally served uses both wheat and rice flours. A gluten-free baguette with rice flour would also work quite well. *See photo, page 83.*

To make the pickled vegetables, using a julienne slicer or a sharp knife, cut the carrots into long matchsticks. With a mandoline or the same sharp knife, slice the radishes as thinly as possible. Cut the cucumber diagonally into slices about ⅛-inch thick.

Combine the white vinegar, sugar, and salt in a medium bowl, whisking vigorously until the sugar is dissolved, or nearly so. Add the carrots, radishes, and cucumbers. Stir and toss to evenly coat the vegetables. Set aside to pickle for 30 to 60 minutes. Once pickled, drain the vegetables and place them in an airtight container in the refrigerator until you are ready to serve. (You may have pickles left over; they will keep for up to 3 days.)

To make the aïoli, combine the mayonnaise, garlic, and lemon zest in a small bowl. Cover and refrigerate for at least 20 minutes and up to 1 day to allow the flavors to meld.

To prepare the salmon, in a bowl, whisk together the boiling water and the brown sugar, stirring until the sugar dissolves. Add the fish sauce, Sriracha, tamari, and garlic and stir to combine. Set aside about 3 tablespoons of the marinade to drizzle over the sandwiches. Transfer the rest of the marinade to a shallow baking dish and let cool to room temperature. Place the salmon slices in the marinade, turning to coat both sides. Cover and refrigerate for about 1 hour, turning the salmon halfway through.

Preheat the broiler. Remove the salmon from the marinade and place in a shallow dish. Broil 6 inches from the heat source for 6 to 8 minutes, until the salmon is golden brown and crisped at the edges. (Cooking time may be shorter with a thinner fillet.)

To assemble the sandwiches, split a baguette piece and hollow out some of the bread. Spread both cut sides of the inside of the baguette with some of the aioli. Layer the bottom half of the sandwich with a generous quantity of the pickled vegetables, 1 tablespoon of the cilantro, and 1 tablespoon of the basil. Top with one piece of the salmon, breaking it into chunky pieces, and some of the jalapeño slices. Drizzle the salmon with some of the reserved marinade. Top with the baguette top. Repeat with the remaining ingredients to make three more sandwiches and serve immediately.

SERVES 4

PIMM'S CUP

8 ounces (1 cup) Pimm's No. 1

8 ounces (1 cup) strong ginger beer

4 ounces (½ cup) freshly squeezed lemon juice

1½ cups ice

16 small strawberries, hulled and thinly sliced

¼ cup loosely packed fresh mint leaves (such as apple mint or orange mint)

1 small Persian cucumber, thinly sliced into rounds

½ lemon, thinly sliced into rounds

Pimm's Cup is the perfect summer drink. It's refreshing as all get out and filled with lots of bright, summery odds and ends that add textural depth and a lovely fragrance—especially if you go for mint varieties like apple mint, which I used here. I prefer a less sweet Pimm's Cup, loaded with fruit and herbs and using lemon juice instead of lemon soda.

In a large pitcher, combine the Pimm's No. 1, ginger beer, and lemon juice and stir. Add about half of the ice, followed by the strawberries, mint, cucumber, lemon rounds, and remaining ice. Stir gently, then serve immediately. You can make this ahead of time and chill, keeping the ice and fresh ingredients separate until you are ready to serve.

SERVES 4

Summer
SQUASH

SWEET CORN *and* SQUASH FRITTERS *with* AVOCADO CREMA

I can't get enough sweet corn in the summer. I eat it on the cob with salt and butter, tossed into salads, and in lots of fritters. I tire pretty quickly of summer squash, but here it plays an essential role as a binder and builder of structure. The corn makes everything bright with those little bursts of sweetness in every bite. And the crema feels rich and decadent but is nothing more than an avocado blended until creamy with yogurt and a squeeze of lime and salt. Perfect summer eating.

Stand the ears of corn upright in a large bowl. Using a very sharp knife, slowly slice the kernels of corn from the cob and into the bowl. Add the zucchini, yellow squash, jalapeño, green onions, basil, cilantro, and salt. Add the egg and mix until evenly combined. Add ¼ cup of flour, mixing again until combined. If your batter is on the wet side, continue adding flour in 1 tablespoon increments, using no more than ½ cup of flour. The consistency of the batter should be moist, but more vegetable than batter. Set aside to rest for about 10 minutes.

While the batter rests, make the crema by combining the avocado, yogurt, lime juice, and salt in a bowl. Blend with an immersion blender or in a food processor until creamy. Set aside.

In a large heavy skillet over medium heat, heat 1 tablespoon of the olive oil. Working in batches, measure a scant ¼ cup of the batter for each fritter and drop it into the pan, lightly pressing with a spatula. Cook 3 to 4 fritters at a time, undisturbed, for 4 to 5 minutes, until the edges are lightly browned. Flip and cook the other side for about 4 minutes more. Place the fritters on a paper towel–lined plate. Repeat with the remaining batter, adding another tablespoon of oil to the pan at the start of each batch.

Serve the fritters warm, topped with the crema and basil.

MAKES 10 FRITTERS

2 small ears corn, preferably white, husks and silk removed

½ cup grated zucchini

½ cup grated yellow squash (any summer squash will work here)

½ to 1 small jalapeño, seeded and minced

5 green onions, white and pale green parts only, thinly sliced

¼ cup chopped fresh basil

3 tablespoons chopped fresh cilantro

1 teaspoon fine sea salt

1 egg, beaten

¼ to ½ cup all-purpose flour

3 tablespoons extra-virgin olive oil

AVOCADO CREMA

1 avocado, diced

½ cup plain Greek yogurt

1 tablespoon freshly squeezed lime juice

¼ teaspoon fine sea salt

Basil leaves, cut into thin ribbons (chiffonade)

SUMMER SQUASH PASTA *with* GREEN GODDESS DRESSING

2 pounds mixed summer squash (yellow squash and zucchini)

1 teaspoon fine sea salt, plus additional for serving

½ cup plain whole milk Greek yogurt

2 tablespoons extra-virgin olive oil

2 tablespoons freshly squeezed lemon juice

1 tablespoon red wine vinegar

¼ cup chopped fresh basil, plus more for garnish

2 tablespoons chopped fresh flat-leaf parsley

2 tablespoons chopped fresh chives

2 tablespoon chopped fresh tarragon

1 small clove garlic, minced

1 anchovy, minced

¼ cup shaved Parmesan cheese

¼ cup raw pine nuts

Freshly ground black pepper

I love the way these squash noodles behave so similarly to pasta, curling around a fork and making a beautiful, tangled mess. There is an appealing novelty to the noodles—exactly what we need when that surplus of summer squash hits, and we're stumped for new uses. Tossed with a variation on the classic Green Goddess dressing, the salad makes a perfect meal for a hot summer evening, when we should all be outdoors, as far away from the stove as possible.

Cut the squash into very thin strips using a julienne slicer. Alternately, use a vegetable peeler or mandoline to make long ribbons. Sprinkle the squash with the salt, toss gently, and place in a colander over a bowl for 20 minutes, allowing the excess liquid in the squash to drain. Carefully squeeze the squash over the colander. Pat with a clean, absorbent kitchen towel to dry.

Combine the yogurt, olive oil, lemon juice, wine vinegar, basil, parsley, chives, tarragon, garlic, and anchovy in a food processor. Blend until smooth and creamy.

Using your hands, gently toss the squash with about three-quarters of the dressing. Add the Parmesan and pine nuts and toss again. If needed, add the remaining dressing; store any remaining dressing in the fridge for another use.

Season to taste with salt and pepper and garnish with small leaves of basil. This dish is best served immediately.

SERVES 4 TO 6

TOMATOES

SCRAMBLED EGGS *with* CHERRY TOMATOES *and* HARISSA

Harissa is a wonderfully flavorful paste of chiles and spices originally from Tunisia. There are thousands of variations—some of them more mild and savory, some of them tear-inducingly spicy. This harissa falls somewhere in the middle—its heat is assertive, but it won't reduce you to tears. I'm smitten with harissa's rich, smoky flavor and slather it generously on vegetables and fish. I'm also fond of a generous dollop of Greek yogurt on my eggs. Here, the two come together with the concentrated sweetness of cherry tomatoes and soft, creamy scrambled eggs.

To make the harissa, place the chiles and sun-dried tomatoes in a large bowl and cover with boiling water. Cover and let sit until softened, about 30 minutes.

In a dry pan over medium heat, toast the caraway seeds, coriander seeds, and cumin seeds until fragrant and beginning to brown, about 2 minutes, stirring regularly. Finely grind the spices using a mortar and pestle or a spice grinder.

When the chiles and sun-dried tomatoes are soft, drain them. Wearing gloves to protect your hands, remove and discard the seeds and stems of the chiles. Place the chiles and sun-dried tomatoes in a food processor. Add the ground spices, garlic, olive oil, lemon juice, wine vinegar, and salt. Pulse until well combined. Set aside. This recipe will make more harissa than is needed. Refrigerate the extra in a tightly sealed jar, with a thin layer of olive oil drizzled on top, for up to a month.

Whisk the eggs with a pinch each of salt and pepper. In a large skillet over low heat, melt the butter. Add the eggs and cook, pushing them gently toward the center of the pan with a spoon. Keep the eggs moving so that they cook consistently. Remove the pan from the heat just before the eggs are cooked through; they will still look a bit glossy, but will continue to cook. Divide among four plates. Top with a smear of yogurt, a dollop of harissa, and a generous handful of cherry tomatoes. Garnish with flaky sea salt and pepper. Serve hot.

SERVES 4

HARISSA

6 large dried chiles, such as New Mexico or guajillo

6 dried chipotle chiles

8 dry-packed sun-dried tomatoes

1 teaspoon whole caraway seeds

1 teaspoon whole coriander seeds

1 teaspoon whole cumin seeds

1 large clove garlic, minced

¼ cup extra-virgin olive oil

2 tablespoons freshly squeezed lemon juice

2 tablespoons red wine vinegar

1 teaspoon fine sea salt

8 eggs

Fine sea salt

Freshly ground black pepper

1 tablespoon unsalted butter

Plain Greek yogurt, for serving

2 cups halved or quartered cherry tomatoes

Flaky sea salt, such as Maldon, for serving

VIBRANT FOOD

TOMATO FENNEL SOUP
with POLENTA CROUTONS

TOMATO FENNEL SOUP

2 pounds ripe red tomatoes

2 small fennel bulbs
(about 16 ounces)

1 yellow onion, cut into 8 pieces

2 tablespoons extra-virgin olive oil

Fine sea salt

Freshly ground black pepper

3 to 4 cups low-sodium
vegetable broth

2 bay leaves

POLENTA CROUTONS

1 (18-ounce) tube prepared
polenta, preferably organic

1½ tablespoons extra-virgin
olive oil

In San Francisco, our summers are often cool and foggy, so making the most of summer produce while keeping cozy is frequently a goal in my cooking. This soup nails it. The caramelized flavors of the tomato, fennel, and onion lend a rich depth to the soup. The polenta croutons are a playful riff on the thick slice of toast or grilled cheese sandwich so often served with tomato soup. The soup is great on its own, and even better with the croutons. The croutons take a little work, but they're worth the effort. If you're pressed for time, however, classic bread croutons or crackers will do. *See photo, page 99.*

Preheat the oven to 400°F.

To make the soup, hull the tomatoes, halve them crosswise, and remove the seeds. Place on half of a rimmed baking sheet, cut-sides up. Trim the stalks and fronds from the fennel bulbs, reserving some of the fronds for garnish. Quarter each fennel bulb, remove the core, and add to the baking sheet along with the onion pieces. Drizzle the tomatoes with 1 tablespoon of the olive oil. Drizzle the fennel and onion with the remaining 1 tablespoon of olive oil, then toss to coat evenly. Season the vegetables with salt and pepper. Roast, turning the onion and fennel occasionally, until the vegetables are very tender and caramelized, about 40 minutes. Set aside for about 10 minutes to cool slightly.

Working in batches if necessary, transfer the roasted vegetables and their pan juices to a food processor or blender. Add 3 cups of the broth and puree the vegetables until very smooth; add more broth to the soup if needed to achieve the desired consistency.

Transfer the soup to a heavy pot. Add the bay leaves, season with ½ teaspoon salt and pepper to taste, then bring the soup to a boil over medium-high heat. Reduce the heat to medium-low and simmer until the flavors come together, about 15 minutes.

Meanwhile, make the polenta croutons. Remove the polenta from the packaging, trim the ends, and cut it crosswise into eight ½-inch-thick slices. Cut the slices into ½-inch cubes. (Don't worry if the end pieces aren't perfectly square.)

In a large nonstick frying pan over medium-high heat, warm the olive oil until it is nearly smoking. Carefully add the polenta cubes and spread them into a single, even layer—they will sputter and pop as they cook. If your pan is not large enough to spread the polenta cubes into a single layer, you can use two pans or work in batches. Cook, without turning, until a golden brown crust forms on the bottom, 5 to 7 minutes. Using two forks, gently turn the croutons over to brown the opposite side. Cook for another 4 to 5 minutes, until the croutons are golden brown and crispy on two sides.

To serve, ladle the soup into bowls. Garnish each with some of the reserved fennel fronds. Top with some of the polenta croutons just before serving—they will lose their crispness if they sit in the soup too long. Serve immediately.

SERVES 6

GRILLED TROUT *with* GREEN TOMATO RELISH

I have always been intrigued by green tomatoes, especially as the notable American classic, the inimitable fried green tomato. On the rarest of occasions, my mother would fry green tomatoes with some of our surplus from the garden. For this dish, I wanted to capture the essence of a green tomato without dredging it in flour and tossing it in a vat of bubbling oil. And so, a relish. It is deeply green, in every sense of the word: it is fresh and cooling, bright and tart, and a little bit sweet. Try it with hot dogs or corn on the cob, too. Look for an unripe heirloom tomato variety, such as Green Zebra, or try green cherry tomatoes.

To make the relish, in the bowl of a food processor, combine the green tomatoes, parsley, chives, tarragon, capers, olive oil, lemon juice, and salt and pulse until a chunky sauce forms. Taste and season with more salt or lemon juice, if needed. Transfer to a bowl and set aside.

Prepare a charcoal or gas grill for direct grilling over medium heat. Oil the grill grate. Brush the outside skin of the trout with olive oil. Season inside and out with salt. Stuff four lemon slices in the cavity of each trout. Place the trout on the grill directly over the fire and cover. Cook, carefully turning once about halfway through, until the trout is opaque, about 10 minutes.

To serve, divide the frisée among four dinner plates. Season each with a pinch of salt and a squeeze of lemon. Place one whole trout on each plate. Spoon some of the green tomato relish over the trout, and add a few slices of heirloom tomatoes. Serve immediately.

SERVES 4

GREEN TOMATO RELISH

16 ounces unripe green tomatoes, hulled and chopped

1 tablespoon finely chopped fresh flat-leaf parsley

1 tablespoon minced fresh chives

1 tablespoon finely chopped fresh tarragon

1 to 2 tablespoons capers

2 tablespoons extra-virgin olive oil

Juice of 1 large lemon, plus more as needed

½ teaspoon fine sea salt, plus more as needed

4 whole butterflied trout, about 8 ounces each

Extra-virgin olive oil

Fine sea salt

8 thin slices lemon, halved

2 cups coarsely chopped frisée

½ lemon

Sliced heirloom tomatoes, for serving

VIBRANT FOOD

PEPPERS

SMOKY RED PEPPER SOUP
with PUMPKIN SEEDS *and* FETA

3 pounds red bell peppers
(4 to 6 peppers)

1 tablespoon plus 1 teaspoon
extra-virgin olive oil

1 small red onion, diced

2 cloves garlic, minced

1 teaspoon sweet paprika

1 teaspoon smoked paprika

1 teaspoon fine sea salt

¼ teaspoon ground chipotle
chile powder

4 cups low-sodium vegetable broth

¼ cup raw, shelled pumpkin seeds

¼ teaspoon ground cumin

½ cup crumbled feta cheese

I love what fire does to a pepper, making it lusciously smoky and rich. This soup takes the essence of a pepper and concentrates it. Peppers are one of those ingredients whose color is hardly diminished by cooking. I find that I need texture in a blended soup; this one is rounded out with pumpkin seeds toasted in cumin and a few chunks of salty feta cheese.

Preheat the broiler.

Arrange the peppers in a single layer on a baking sheet. Broil 6 to 8 inches from the heat for 15 to 20 minutes, turning every few minutes, until the peppers are mostly blackened. Remove from the broiler and set aside to cool.

When the peppers are cool enough to handle, remove the skins under running water. Pull the stems from the peppers and rinse out the seeds. Coarsely chop the peppers and set aside.

Warm 1 tablespoon of the oil in a large stockpot. Add the onions and sauté for 3 minutes, stirring occasionally. Add the garlic and sauté for another minute. Stir in the sweet and smoked paprika, salt, and chipotle powder. Add the broth and the red peppers and bring to a boil. Reduce the heat to low, cover, and simmer for 15 minutes.

In a small pan over medium heat, add the remaining 1 teaspoon of olive oil. Add the pumpkin seeds and the cumin and sauté until toasted, 3 to 4 minutes, stirring regularly. Set aside.

Purée the soup using an immersion blender or food processor. To serve, top each bowl with the toasted pumpkin seeds and crumbled feta cheese.

SERVES 4

MILLET-STUFFED PEPPERS
with TOMATILLO SALSA

Stuffed peppers are pretty fantastic in all of their forms. I enjoy using a variety of other grains as an alternative to rice to stuff them—and so, the millet used here. This dish really comes to life when you use a small, sweet variety of pepper or an heirloom pepper variety instead of a bell pepper. They tend to have a more intense flavor, which I prefer.

In a saucepan over medium-low heat, warm 1 tablespoon of the olive oil. Add the onion and sauté, stirring, until soft, 3 to 5 minutes. Add the millet and toast until very lightly browned and fragrant, 3 to 4 minutes. Add the tomato and broth and bring to a boil. Reduce the heat and simmer, covered, for 15 minutes. Turn off the heat and let stand for 10 minutes.

While the millet is cooking, stand the ear of corn upright in a large, wide bowl. Using a very sharp knife, slowly slice the kernels of corn away from the cob and into the bowl. Set aside.

Preheat the oven to 400°F. Line a large baking sheet with parchment paper.

When the millet is cooked, gently fluff it with a fork. Stir in the corn, Monterey Jack, remaining 1 tablespoon of olive oil, salt, paprika, chili powder, and pepper to taste. To stuff the peppers, make a long slit from stem to tip. If there are a lot of seeds or a thick membrane, carefully remove. Using a small spoon, stuff each pepper with the millet mixture. Place them on the baking sheet, spaced slightly apart so they don't steam while baking. You may have a little leftover millet, depending on the size of your peppers. Bake the peppers for 20 to 25 minutes, depending on their size, until cooked through and beginning to brown.

While the peppers cook, make the tomatillo salsa. Remove the husks from the tomatillos, rinse them thoroughly (they are very sticky), and coarsely chop. Combine the tomatillos, avocado, green onions, serrano, cilantro, lime juice, and salt in a food processor and process until coarsely blended.

To serve, spoon the tomatillo salsa over the peppers, and finish by sprinkling the queso fresco and additional cilantro on top.

2 tablespoons extra-virgin olive oil

½ yellow onion, diced

¾ cup millet

1 small tomato, diced

1¼ cups low-sodium vegetable broth

1 ear fresh corn, husks and silk removed

1 cup coarsely grated Monterey Jack cheese

1 teaspoon fine sea salt

½ teaspoon sweet paprika

¼ teaspoon ground chili powder

Freshly ground black pepper

16 ounces small sweet peppers

Queso fresco, for serving

TOMATILLO SALSA

8 ounces tomatillos

½ avocado

3 green onions, white and pale green parts only, thinly sliced

1 serrano chile, seeded and minced

¼ cup chopped fresh cilantro, plus more for garnish

Juice of 1½ limes

¼ teaspoon fine sea salt

FALL

The RICH COLORS *of* FALL

FALL is the season where the landscape most strongly mirrors the produce. It is dominated by the colors of the harvest—a wash of golds, reds, oranges, and yellows, all tawny and burnished and warm. The beginning of the season is summer's last hurrah—tomatoes, peppers, and summer squash, and even peaches, plums, and melons hang on into late September. The nights cool and lengthen, and warm and comforting foods come into their own. Winter squash, such as delicata, acorn, and kabocha, burst onto the scene with orange and golden and green hues in the fall (and, true to their name, will keep into the winter). Apples and pears taste their best right now, and there are so many gorgeous heirloom varieties to be excited by. The first of the brussels sprouts, cauliflower, and kale are kind of exciting at this time of year, before the long winter when we're so anxious for spring's color and bright produce.

VIBRANT FOOD

GRAPES

WILD RICE SALAD
with RAINBOW CHARD
and GRAPES

½ cup wild rice

1½ cups water

½ teaspoon fine sea salt

1 cup red grapes, sliced in half lengthwise

1 tablespoon balsamic vinegar

1 teaspoon chopped fresh rosemary, plus more for garnish

1 bunch rainbow chard

1 tablespoon extra-virgin olive oil

½ cup raw hazelnuts

½ cup crumbled feta cheese

BALSAMIC VINAIGRETTE

2 tablespoons balsamic vinegar

1 tablespoon extra-virgin olive oil

1 tablespoon minced shallot

½ teaspoon chopped fresh rosemary

¼ teaspoon Dijon mustard

¼ teaspoon fine sea salt

Freshly ground black pepper

This hearty salad is an homage to the harvest: Both wild rice and grapes peak in the golden days of September and October. Rainbow chard adds a leafy tang, and the feta and hazelnuts keep it from being just another healthy grain salad. It's rich, hearty, and perfectly filling—and it stands well on its own as a simple meal.

In a small heavy pot, combine the wild rice, water, and ¼ teaspoon of the salt. Bring to a boil, then reduce the heat to low and cover. Simmer over low heat for 50 to 60 minutes, until the water is absorbed and the rice has puffed open.

Preheat the oven to 350°. While the rice cooks, toast the nuts. Arrange the hazelnuts in a single layer on a baking sheet. Toast until golden brown and fragrant, 8 to 10 minutes. Set aside to cool for about 5 minutes, then coarsely chop.

Next, combine the grapes with the balsamic vinegar, rosemary, and the remaining ¼ teaspoon salt. Set aside to marinate, tossing occasionally.

Slice the chard stems from the leaves using a sharp knife. Slice the stems into small disks. Chop the chard leaves coarsely. Keep the stems and leaves separate.

Heat the olive oil in a large skillet over medium-low heat. Add the chard stems and sauté for about 2 minutes to soften. Add the chard leaves and stir constantly until the leaves are soft, another 3 minutes or so. Remove from the heat, drain off any excess liquid, and set aside to cool for 5 to 10 minutes.

To prepare the vinaigrette, whisk together the balsamic vinegar, olive oil, shallot, rosemary, mustard, and salt. Add black pepper to taste.

In a large bowl, toss the cooked rice, chard, and grapes with the vinaigrette. Divide the salad among plates, and top with hazelnuts and feta. Garnish with rosemary. Serve at room temperature.

SERVES 4 TO 6

CONCORD GRAPE
and MINT SORBET

The foxy flavor and intensely purple hue of the Concord grape make for a
refreshing sorbet in the golden days of September and October. It's a time
of year when San Francisco often sees its best weather, with warm days
and softly glowing clear skies. It's a beautiful moment, one that needs a
little celebratory treat to welcome the harvest. If you haven't invested in an
ice cream maker yet, I highly recommend seeking one out. They're pretty
inexpensive and your reward is something like this—a gorgeous-colored,
fruit-forward sorbet in homage to the season.

¼ cup agave nectar

¼ cup water

3 tablespoons fresh, chopped
mint leaves

2 pounds fresh Concord grapes,
stems removed

Juice of 1 lime

To make a mint simple syrup, combine the agave nectar, water, and mint in a
small saucepan over medium heat, stirring regularly, until almost simmering,
about 3 to 5 minutes. Remove the pan from the heat and allow the syrup to
cool to room temperature, at least 30 minutes.

Using a food processor or blender, puree the grapes until smooth. Strain the
grape mixture through a fine-mesh strainer, pressing any remaining juices with
a spatula. Add the mint simple syrup and the lime juice and stir. Cover the
mixture and chill until very cold, at least 3 hours.

Remove the sorbet mixture from the fridge. Churn the sorbet in an ice
cream maker for about 25 to 30 minutes, or according to the manufacturer's
instructions, until frozen. The sorbet will still be soft. Place in the freezer for
at least 3 hours more to freeze completely. Transfer to an airtight container if
not serving immediately.

SERVES 6

FIGS

TURKEY BURGERS
with BALSAMIC FIGS

These turkey burgers were inspired by the cheese and chutney sandwiches that I fondly recall eating on a train ride in England as a kid. They were so strange to me then; pairing jam and cheese in a sandwich was something my parents would have never served us. I borrowed some of the elements of a chutney in building the marinated figs: there's the acid from the vinegar, a touch of heat from the red pepper flakes, and a little sweetness from the agave. I prefer a burger that is made with lots of herbs—it feels healthier to eat a burger that has almost as much produce as it does protein.

To prepare the figs, whisk together the olive oil, balsamic vinegar, mustard, agave nectar, salt, and red pepper flakes. Add the figs, green onions, and mint; toss gently to combine. Set aside.

To make the burgers, heat 1 tablespoon of the olive oil in a skillet over medium-low heat. Add the onion and sauté, stirring, until soft and translucent but not yet beginning to brown, about 5 minutes.

In a large bowl, combine the onion, turkey, apple, parsley, thyme, salt, and black pepper and mix by hand until just combined, being careful not to overmix. Divide the burger mixture into four equal parts and form into patties about ¾-inch thick.

Add 1 tablespoon of the olive oil to a large skillet over medium heat. Cook two to three patties at a time—you don't want to crowd them. Cook without disturbing for 5 to 6 minutes, then flip. About 2 minutes into cooking the second side, place the cheddar slices on top of the burgers, cover the skillet, and cook for 1 to 2 minutes more to melt the cheese. Repeat with the remaining patties.

While the burgers cook, toast the buns.

To serve, place the greens on the bottom half of each bun, followed by a burger and a large, generous spoonful of the balsamic fig mixture.

SERVES 4

BALSAMIC FIGS

2 tablespoons extra-virgin olive oil

1 tablespoon balsamic vinegar

1 tablespoon whole-grain Dijon mustard

1 teaspoon agave nectar

¼ teaspoon fine sea salt

¼ teaspoon dried red pepper flakes

6 small fresh figs, sliced lengthwise into ¼-inch slices

3 green onions, white and pale green parts only, thinly sliced

1 tablespoon small fresh mint leaves

TURKEY BURGERS

3 tablespoons extra-virgin olive oil

½ small yellow onion, finely diced

16 ounces ground turkey

¼ large apple, cored and finely diced

2 tablespoons chopped fresh flat-leaf parsley

2 teaspoons fresh thyme

¾ teaspoon fine sea salt

Freshly ground black pepper

4 large slices sharp cheddar cheese

4 burger buns

Mixed greens

BROILED FIGS *with* ZA'ATAR *and* PECANS

ZA'ATAR

1 teaspoon sesame seeds

1 teaspoon dried thyme

1 teaspoon sumac

¼ teaspoon fine sea salt

½ cup raw, chopped pecans

12 large fresh figs, halved lengthwise

¼ cup honey

Vanilla ice cream or fromage blanc, for serving

Pairing sweet and savory flavors is among my favorite techniques, and za'atar—the Middle Eastern spice blend most often composed of wild thyme, sumac, and sesame seeds—is a dynamic match with the figs. The sumac and figs cast a faint purple stain on the honey, which is lovely when drizzled over ice cream or a tangy soft cheese like fromage blanc. Use a store-bought za'atar mix if you can't find sumac.

Preheat the broiler.

To make the za'atar, combine the sesame seeds, thyme, sumac, and salt in a bowl. Toss with the pecans and set aside.

Place the figs cut side up in a small roasting pan. Using a small spoon, carefully drizzle the honey over the figs. Broil 6 inches from the heat for 5 minutes. Remove from the broiler and sprinkle the za'atar mix over the figs. Return to the broiler for another 1 to 2 minutes, until the pecans are toasted.

Allow the figs to cool for a couple of minutes. Serve warm, with vanilla ice cream or fromage blanc and a little of the remaining honey drizzled on top.

SERVES 4 TO 6

VIBRANT FOOD

Tree
FRUITS

APPLE SAGE WALNUT BREAD

It's in the cool days of fall that I find myself craving a sweet, snacky treat most often. Sage adds an intriguing, savory herbal note to the sweetness and warmth of this most autumnal of breads. I use fleeting Pink Pearl apples because I am so tickled by their pink interior, but any firm, sweet-tart apple will work. There's no need to peel the apples before baking; the skins add a little textural depth and subtle streaks of pink throughout the cake. You can easily make your own oat flour by pulsing rolled oats in a food processor.

Preheat the oven to 350°F. Butter and flour an 8-inch square pan. Set aside.

In a large mixing bowl, combine the brown rice and oat flours, brown sugar, baking powder, baking soda, salt, cinnamon, and nutmeg and whisk until blended.

In a separate bowl, thoroughly whisk together the eggs, olive oil, yogurt, and applesauce. Fold the wet ingredients into the dry until combined. Gently mix in the diced apples. The batter will be quite thick, especially if you are using all-purpose flour.

To prepare the topping, in a bowl, mix together the oats, walnuts, flour, brown sugar, sage, cinnamon, nutmeg, and salt. Using your fingers, work in the butter until the mixture is well combined.

Pour the batter into the prepared pan and smooth the top. Sprinkle the crumble topping evenly over the batter.

Bake for 45 to 50 minutes, until a toothpick inserted in the center of the bread comes out clean. Transfer to a wire rack to cool for about 10 minutes before serving.

SERVES 8 TO 10

1 cup brown rice flour
(or use all-purpose flour)

1 cup oat flour (or use all-purpose)

1 cup lightly packed brown sugar

1 teaspoon baking powder

½ teaspoon baking soda

½ teaspoon fine sea salt

1 teaspoon ground cinnamon

¼ teaspoon ground nutmeg

2 eggs, lightly beaten

6 tablespoons extra-virgin olive oil

⅓ cup plain whole milk
Greek yogurt

¼ cup applesauce

2 small red apples, cored and
diced (about 1½ cups)

⅓ cup rolled oats

⅓ cup coarsely chopped walnuts

3 tablespoons oat flour
(or use all-purpose flour)

¼ cup lightly packed brown sugar

2½ tablespoons chopped
fresh sage

¼ teaspoon ground cinnamon

¼ teaspoon ground nutmeg

¼ teaspoon fine sea salt

3 tablespoons cold unsalted
butter, cubed

CARNITAS TACOS
with APPLE SALSA

This is my riff on carnitas. It's also my riff on pork and apples. I experimented with a few different fall and winter fruits for the salsa: citrus, Asian pear, and apples. In this context, the apple salsa was the hands-down winner. It's a lovely counterpart to the deep flavors and crispy texture of the pork—something bright and fresh to balance all of that rich, succulent meat.

To make the carnitas, in a large mixing bowl, combine the ancho and chipotle chile powders, cumin, salt, and pepper. Toss the pork into the bowl and generously coat with the dry rub.

In a large, heavy pot, such as a Dutch oven, warm the oil over medium-high heat. Add as many cubes of pork as will fit in a single layer and sear until browned on all sides, turning occasionally, about 15 minutes. Transfer the browned meat to a bowl and repeat with the remaining pork.

When all of the pork is browned, add the onion, garlic, orange juice, and water to the pot, along with any pork that was removed. Cover and bring to a boil. Reduce the heat to low and cook until the pork is falling-apart tender and cooked through, about 1½ hours.

Remove the lid. Using tongs or a large fork, pull the pork apart to shred it. Raise the heat and cook, uncovered, until the liquid reduces and the meat begins to brown and crisp at the edges, 25 to 30 minutes.

While the pork cooks, make the salsa. In a mixing bowl, toss together the apple, green onions, cilantro, jalapeño, salt, and lime juice until well combined. Set aside until you are ready to serve.

To serve, top each warm tortilla with pulled pork, apple salsa, cabbage, and queso fresco. Garnish with additional cilantro and serve with lime wedges on the side.

SERVES 6 TO 8

CARNITAS

2 teaspoons ancho chile powder

2 teaspoons chipotle chile powder

2 teaspoons ground cumin

2 teaspoons fine sea salt

½ teaspoon freshly ground black pepper

3 pounds boneless pork shoulder, cut into 3-inch pieces

1 tablespoon extra-virgin olive oil

1 yellow onion, quartered

4 garlic cloves, smashed

Juice of 1 orange

2 cups water

APPLE SALSA

1 large, sweet-tart red apple, such as Braeburn or Pink Lady, cored and finely diced

6 green onions, white and pale green parts only, thinly sliced

¼ cup coarsely chopped fresh cilantro, plus more for garnish

1 jalapeño, seeded and finely minced

½ teaspoon fine sea salt

Juice of 2 limes

12 to 16 corn tortillas, warmed

1 to 2 cups shredded red cabbage

1 cup crumbled queso fresco

Lime wedges

MULLED WHITE WINE

1 (750 ml) bottle dry, fruity white wine, such as a dry Riesling or Viognier

2 tablespoons honey

6 green cardamom pods

2 cinnamon sticks

2 star anise pods

2 large slices ginger

½ teaspoon black peppercorns

1 firm red pear, such as Starkrimson, cored and thinly sliced

There was one chilly fall and winter in my life during which I sometimes microwaved a mug of white wine mixed with cinnamon and apple juice on cold nights. It sounds kind of tacky, right? But it was really delicious. I don't think that I truly understood what mulling meant then, or its value in slowly bringing out the essence of the spices in a warm pot of wine. But I won't judge if you decide to cut corners and make a mug of warmed wine in the microwave. We all have our moments.

In a pot over low heat, warm the wine and honey. Once the honey is dissolved, add the cardamom pods, cinnamon sticks, star anise, ginger, and peppercorns. Mull, covered, over the lowest heat for about 30 minutes, being careful to not let the mixture boil.

To serve, divide the wine among 4 to 6 mugs. Add one or two slices of red pear to each mug. Garnish with some of the spices used to mull the wine, if desired. Serve warm.

You can prepare the wine a day in advance. If you do, don't add the ginger and black pepper until you are rewarming to serve.

SERVES 4 TO 6

ALMOND HONEY CAKE
with POACHED QUINCE

POACHED QUINCES

5 cups water

1 cup natural cane sugar

5 green cardamom pods

Juice of 1 lemon

1 teaspoon black peppercorns

4 quinces

ALMOND HONEY CAKE

2 cups almond flour

1 teaspoon baking powder

½ teaspoon baking soda

1½ teaspoons ground cardamom

½ teaspoon fine sea salt

3 eggs, beaten

⅔ cup honey

¼ cup extra-virgin olive oil

Zest of 1 orange

Confectioners' sugar

½ cup chopped raw pistachios

Quinces can sometimes intimidate people, but they shouldn't. Aside from the fuss of getting them peeled and cut (which is why it's best to do one big batch so that you have leftovers), they're incredibly versatile and lovely in just about anything where a poached pear or bit of warm fruit would be welcome— whether that's your morning granola or your favorite cake. They turn the most incredible shade of dusty pink after long poaching, and, perhaps most importantly, cooked quinces possess an unparalleled fragrance that's vaguely rosy and absolutely intoxicating. Flourless almond cakes have a denseness to them that I adore—it's an entirely different beast than a fluffy white cake. The quince syrup from the poaching liquid is what brings this all together— it lends a little moisture and a sweet tang to the cake, which absorbs it readily. If quinces are out of season or unavailable, try this with macerated berries or poached figs. *See photo, page 135.*

To poach the quinces, bring the water, sugar, cardamom pods, lemon juice, and peppercorns to a gentle boil in a heavy covered pot.

While the water comes to a boil, prepare the quinces. They are stubborn and challenging, so work with a very sharp knife and be patient. Peel the outer skins. Slice the quinces into quarters, and carefully core them. Slice each quarter into thirds lengthwise, so that each fruit is divided into twelve pieces. Put the slices in the simmering liquid to prevent browning.

Once you've added all of the quinces to the pot, cover, reduce the heat to low, and simmer for about 1½ hours, until the quinces are soft and have turned a rosy pink. Remove from the heat and cool to room temperature. Store the quinces in their cooking liquid in the fridge until ready to use. They will continue to turn a deeper shade of pink.

While the quinces are cooking, make the almond cake. Preheat the oven to 325°F. Grease a round 9-inch pan with butter and dust with almond flour.

In a large mixing bowl, whisk together the almond flour, baking powder, baking soda, cardamom, and salt.

In another bowl, whisk together the eggs, honey, olive oil, and orange zest. Fold the wet ingredients into the dry, mixing until just combined. Pour the batter into the pan.

Bake for 35 to 40 minutes, until the cake is golden brown and a toothpick inserted in the center comes out clean. Place the cake pan on a wire rack to cool to room temperature.

To make a syrup, pour 2 cups of the quince cooking liquid (this should be about half of the liquid) into a small pot. (The other half can be used for the Quince Cocktail, page 138.) Bring to a boil over medium-high heat. Boil gently until the liquid has reduced to ½ cup, 25 to 30 minutes. Set aside to cool.

To serve, slice the cake into eight pieces. Drizzle each slice with a little of the quince syrup, then dust with confectioners' sugar. Finish with a handful of quince slices tucked around the cake and a sprinkle of chopped pistachios.

SERVES 8

QUINCE COCKTAIL

16 ounces (2 cups) reserved quince poaching liquid from the Poached Quinces (page 136)

6 ounces (¾ cup) bourbon

½ cup freshly squeezed lemon juice

12 dashes Angostura bitters

16 mint leaves, lightly crushed

4 orange twists

I made this cocktail on a whim. There was leftover poaching liquid from the Almond Honey Cake, and adding booze seemed like an obvious next step. It's kinda wonderful—the poaching liquid is charmingly rose-colored, a quality unique to quince, and it's partnered to good effect with some citrus, bitters, and whiskey.

In a pitcher, mix the quince poaching liquid, bourbon, lemon juice, and Angostura bitters. Add 12 of the mint leaves and muddle. Chill for at least 1 hour before serving.

To serve, pour into coupe glasses. Garnish each drink with an orange twist and a mint leaf.

SERVES 4

PERSIMMONS

AUTUMN BREAKFAST BOWL

This is for the oatmeal naysayers. I love oatmeal on a cold morning, but sometimes I struggle with its soft, one-note texture. So I made this as a means of electrifying the gruel, if you will: You'll find texture and flavor and crunch in abundance. I'm partial to Fuyu persimmons, the variety that is firm when ripe. Their flavor is intensely sweet with a faint whiff of spice, and their texture similar to an Asian pear—a little crunchy and quite juicy. They offer a great pop of color.

In a small saucepan, combine the water, oats, cardamom, cinnamon, and salt. Bring to a boil. Lower the heat and simmer, stirring occasionally, until the oats are tender and the water is absorbed, 5 to 7 minutes.

While the oats are cooking, toast the pumpkin seeds and quinoa in a dry pan over medium heat until golden, about 3 minutes, stirring regularly. Remove the pumpkin seeds and quinoa from the pan and set aside to cool.

When the oats are finished, remove them from the heat and divide between two bowls. Top each serving with sliced persimmon, dried cranberries, crystallized ginger, and the toasted pumpkin seeds and quinoa. Add a drizzle of honey if you like your oatmeal on the sweeter side. Serve warm.

SERVES 2

2 cups water

1 cup old-fashioned rolled oats

¼ teaspoon ground cardamom

¼ teaspoon ground cinnamon

Big pinch of fine sea salt

¼ cup raw, shelled pumpkin seeds

2 tablespoons quinoa

1 Fuyu persimmon, quartered and thinly sliced (or substitute apple)

¼ cup dried cranberries

1 tablespoon chopped crystallized ginger

Honey, for serving (optional)

PERSIMMON *with* BROILED GOAT CHEESE

4 ounces soft, fresh goat cheese

1 tablespoon extra-virgin olive oil

Fine sea salt and freshly ground black pepper

2 Fuyu persimmons, quartered, seeded, and thinly sliced

Fresh thyme, for garnish

This is inspired by a dish that I love to serve as an appetizer in the fall. Often I'll just serve slices of firm Fuyu persimmon with plain goat cheese—that alone is tasty enough to surprise and intrigue guests. But I decided to fancify it a little by broiling the goat cheese, which makes it a warm, melty, tangy, wonderful thing. It's really important to select firm Fuyu persimmons for this dish. Soft Hachiya persimmons are unripe when firm, and once ripe, they won't support a slather of cheese as an appetizer.

Preheat the broiler.

Place the goat cheese in a ramekin and drizzle the olive oil over the cheese. Sprinkle with salt and pepper. Broil about 6 inches from the heat source for 8 to 10 minutes, until the cheese is a deep golden brown. Allow to cool for a couple minutes.

Spread about a teaspoon of baked goat cheese on each slice of persimmon. Garnish with thyme and black pepper and serve immediately.

SERVES 4 TO 6

Sturdy Fall
GREENS

WILD MUSHROOM
and GREENS FRITTATA

I love the flexibility of a frittata. It's a welcome and forgiving vehicle for all of those leftovers in the fridge—the last handful of greens, or a bit of broccoli. Here, broccoli di cicco, an heirloom broccoli whose leaves and stems are more tender than our more familiar broccoli, is paired with baby chard, which is milder than mature chard leaves. The rich flavors of wild mushrooms sautéed in butter are the perfect foil to the bracing flavors of the greens. I really enjoy using kefir in place of milk—it's gentler on my belly, and I love its bright, tangy flavor. You can find plain kefir at many natural foods stores.

8 ounces assorted mushrooms, such as chanterelle, cremini, or king trumpet

10 eggs, beaten

4 ounces soft, fresh goat cheese, crumbled

1 tablespoon chopped fresh thyme, plus more for garnish

½ teaspoon fine sea salt

Freshly ground black pepper

¼ cup kefir or buttermilk

2 tablespoons unsalted butter

1 cup coarsely chopped broccoli di cicco

1 cup loosely packed baby chard leaves, plus more for garnish

---

Preheat the oven to 375°F.

Clean the mushrooms using as little water as possible, because washing mushrooms causes them to absorb water and dilutes their flavor. Slice them about ¼ to ½ inch thick.

In a large mixing bowl, whisk the eggs with the kefir, goat cheese, thyme, salt, and pepper. Set aside.

Warm a 10-inch cast-iron or oven-safe skillet over medium-low heat. Add 1 tablespoon of the butter. When it is frothy, add the mushrooms and stir. Sauté them until soft and cooked through, 8 to 10 minutes. Remove the mushrooms from the pan and set aside. In the same pan, add the remaining 1 tablespoon of butter along with the broccoli di cicco and sauté. After 2 or 3 minutes, add the baby chard. Stir until the greens are just soft, 1 or 2 minutes more. Add the mushrooms and egg mixture to the pan, and stir to incorporate everything. Keep the frittata over medium-low heat until the edges begin to firm, 10 to 12 minutes.

Transfer the skillet to the oven to finish cooking, about 10 minutes more, until the eggs are set and golden brown at the edges. Remove the frittata from the oven and set aside to cool for about 5 minutes.

Garnish with a handful of chopped greens and thyme. Serve warm.

SERVES 4 TO 6

CELEBRATION SALAD

1 bunch Tuscan kale, stemmed and sliced into ribbons (chiffonade) (about 8 cups)

1 cup raw walnuts

1 small head radicchio, cored and sliced into ribbons (chiffonade)

1 cup crumbled feta, preferably French

1 small red pear, such as Starkrimson, cored and thinly sliced lengthwise

1 heaping cup pomegranate seeds

5 tablespoons extra-virgin olive oil

2 tablespoons balsamic vinegar

1 teaspoon Dijon mustard

1 small clove garlic, minced

Fine sea salt and freshly ground black pepper

This salad was born from a mess. I was working on a big project with the help of my friend Stacy. Lunchtime was upon us and amid all the piles of chopped vegetables, we found the beginnings of a kitchen sink salad. So I sautéed some kale, tossed it in balsamic vinegar, added some leftover pear, toasted walnuts, pomegranates, and feta, and a delicious salad came to life. It's a celebration of many things: a glorious pause from work in the middle of the day, the festivities of the season, and that brief window when all of this produce is in season at the same time.

Preheat the oven to 350°F.

In a large mixing bowl, toss the kale with the lemon juice. Set aside, tossing by hand every 10 minutes, for about 30 minutes.

Arrange the walnuts in a single layer on a baking sheet. Toast until golden brown and fragrant, about 8 to 10 minutes. Set aside to cool for about 5 minutes, then coarsely chop.

To prepare the dressing, whisk together the olive oil, balsamic vinegar, mustard, honey, and minced garlic with salt and pepper to taste.

In a large mixing bowl, toss the radicchio and kale together with the dressing, and let stand for 10 minutes.

Transfer the kale and radicchio to a large serving bowl. Top with the walnuts, feta, pear slices, and pomegranate seeds. This salad is best served immediately.

SERVES 6 TO 8

BROILED SALMON *with* CARAMELIZED ONIONS *and* MUSTARD GREENS

1 tablespoon extra-virgin olive oil

1 large red onion, thinly sliced crosswise

¼ teaspoon fine sea salt, plus more to taste

4 (4-ounce) wild salmon fillets

Freshly ground black pepper

1 tablespoon whole-grain Dijon mustard

2 cups chopped baby mustard leaves

If you can find them, baby mustard greens are the friendlier, tamer version of the spicy mustard leaf. And onions, of course, melt into a soft, voluptuous mess when caramelized—it's a wonderfully sweet, faintly spicy pile of goodness atop a broiled salmon fillet. I always purchase wild salmon fillets because the fish are healthier, higher in good fats, and led the athletic life that they were meant to lead in the ocean. It's more expensive than farmed salmon, which is often labeled Atlantic salmon, but farmed salmon is raised in overcrowded conditions, undernourished, and dosed with antibiotics, which is detrimental not only to our own health but also the health of the ocean.

To caramelize the onion, in a large skillet over low heat, warm the olive oil. Add the onion and ¼ teaspoon salt and stir. Cover and sauté over low heat until the onions are soft and jammy, about 40 minutes, stirring every 5 minutes or so.

Meanwhile, preheat the broiler. Lightly grease a medium baking dish. Place the salmon skin side down in the dish. Generously sprinkle with salt and pepper.

After the onions have been cooking for about 30 minutes, place the salmon under the broiler 6 to 8 inches from the heat source. Broil for 5 to 7 minutes, depending on the thickness of the fillet, until beginning to crisp and brown at the edges. Set aside to rest. Remove the salmon skin from the fillet, if desired.

When the onions are just about ready, after 35 to 40 minutes of cooking, add 1 cup of the mustard greens and stir until wilted, about 1 minute. Turn off the heat and stir in the mustard.

To serve, divide the remaining 1 cup of baby mustard leaves among four plates, followed by the salmon and a generous spoonful of the onion jam. Serve immediately.

SERVES 4

Winter
SQUASH

CHILE-ROASTED DELICATA SQUASH *with* QUESO FRESCO

Delicata is my favorite of the winter squash. It's sweeter and, as its name implies, more delicate than other squash. Plus, you don't have to peel it. I enjoy the graceful scalloped edges that are made when you slice through the squash crosswise. The simple combination of smoky chipotle powder, fresh cilantro, and queso fresco perfectly balances the caramelized squash.

Preheat the oven to 400°F.

Slice the squash in half crosswise. Scoop out the seeds and pulp, discarding the pulp. Rinse the seeds and set aside to drain. Slice each squash half into ¼-inch to ½-inch rounds.

In a large mixing bowl, combine the 3 tablespoons olive oil, maple syrup, cumin, chipotle powder, paprika, and salt. Add the squash and toss to thoroughly coat. Arrange the squash in a single layer on a large baking sheet, overlapping the slices slightly if necessary.

On a separate baking sheet, toss the squash seeds with the remaining 1 teaspoon of olive oil and a light sprinkle of salt.

Place the squash and seeds in the oven. Roast the squash for 20 to 25 minutes, turning the slices halfway. Check on the seeds after 10 minutes and remove from the oven when golden brown. The squash will be ready when fork-tender, golden brown, and caramelized.

Place the squash on a large serving dish. Sprinkle the toasted seeds, queso fresco, and cilantro leaves over the squash. This dish is best served warm.

SERVES 4

2 delicata squash
(about 1½ pounds)

3 tablespoons plus 1 teaspoon
extra-virgin olive oil

1 tablespoon maple syrup

½ teaspoon ground cumin

¼ to ½ teaspoon chipotle chile
powder

¼ teaspoon sweet paprika

¼ teaspoon fine sea salt, plus
more to taste

¼ cup crumbled queso fresco

2 tablespoons coarsely chopped
fresh cilantro

SOBA NOODLES *with* KABOCHA SQUASH *in a* MELLOW JAPANESE CURRY

1 small kabocha squash
(about 2 pounds)

3 tablespoons unsalted butter

½ large yellow onion, halved
and thinly sliced

1 large clove garlic, minced

1 tablespoon freshly grated ginger
(or 1 teaspoon dried ginger)

1 teaspoon fine sea salt, plus
more to taste

3 tablespoons brown rice flour

2 tablespoons curry powder

1 tablespoon tomato paste

2 teaspoons honey

4 cups low-sodium vegetable broth

1 cup full-fat coconut milk

1 sweet-tart red apple, cored
and grated

2 large carrots, sliced into
½-inch pieces

8 to 10 ounces dried soba noodles

Extra-virgin olive oil

¼ cup thinly sliced green onions,
for garnish

Micro greens, for garnish
(optional)

I used to work in San Francisco's tiny Japantown. There was a small, well-stocked Japanese market around the corner from our building where many of us would make a ritual of picking up sushi or other prepared foods from their deli. This is where I learned about Japanese curry, a mellower take on the Indian version. Japanese curry is often flavored with ketchup or tonkatsu sauce to sweeten it. Here, I used tomato paste and the natural sweetness of the squash, along with apples and carrots, to lend a sweet flavor without relying on an overly sugary sauce. This is a deeply rich and warming curry that's perfect for a blustery fall day. You can also serve it over rice instead of soba noodles. I use 100 percent buckwheat noodles to keep this dish gluten-free. They're a little less pliable than noodles made with wheat, so add a generous glug of oil to the water when cooking them to keep them separated and pliant. *See photo, page 159.*

Using a very sharp knife, slice the the squash in half. Remove the seeds and fibers and discard. Slice the halves again, and then dice the squash into bite-size pieces, about 1 inch thick. You don't need to peel the squash.

In a large pot over medium heat, melt the butter. Add the onion, garlic, and ginger, and season with a pinch of salt. Sauté until the onion is soft, about 5 minutes, stirring frequently.

Sprinkle the brown rice flour over the onion and cook for 2 minutes more, stirring constantly. Add the curry powder and stir until well combined. Add the tomato paste, honey, and 1 teaspoon salt. The mixture will be very thick and paste-like. Slowly add 1 cup vegetable broth, stirring constantly until smooth. Add the remaining 3 cups of vegetable broth and the coconut milk and combine thoroughly. Add the apple, carrots, and squash. Bring the mixture to a boil, reduce the heat to low, cover, and simmer gently until the vegetables are tender, 25 to 30 minutes. Taste and season with additional salt, if desired.

When the curry is about 15 minutes from being done, fill a pot two-thirds full of salted water and bring to a boil over high heat. Add the soba noodles and a glug of olive oil and cook until tender, about 5 minutes, or according to package directions. Drain the noodles and divide among six to eight soup bowls.

Ladle the hot curry over the noodles, garnish with green onions and micro greens, and serve immediately.

SERVES 6

WINTER

The DEEP COLORS *of* WINTER

EVERYTHING seems to take a pause in the winter, a long sleep. I love the quiet, unexpected places one finds color: in a turnip's faint purple blush, or the deep purple mottling of a rutabaga, or the ruddy orange-pink colors of a sweet potato, or those bright pink-ringed Chioggias. This is winter's secret.

Winter is the most challenging season where produce is concerned. I've made an effort to offer creative, inspiring recipes here that will capture and keep your interest in these darker months. The bright jewel colors of citrus are the one exception to an otherwise muted palette. Citrus is winter's gem, and I am convinced that there are mood-boosting powers in their colors and bright flavors.

Winter
ROOTS

TWICE-BAKED
SWEET POTATOES

2 medium-large sweet potatoes
(about 12 ounces each)

1 tablespoon extra-virgin olive oil

½ yellow onion, diced

¾ cup stemmed and chopped
Tuscan kale

¼ cup plain Greek yogurt

¼ cup freshly grated Parmesan
cheese

2 teaspoons chopped fresh thyme

½ teaspoon fine sea salt

½ cup crumbled feta cheese

My friend Britt brought a version of this dish to a Thanksgiving potluck, and it was a hit. I'm always enthusiastic about novel ways to reinvent comfort food, especially when the vegetable content is boosted. The sweet potato is a great stand-in for a regular potato here, and the kale adds hearty structure to this rich, lovely dish.

Preheat the oven to 400°F.

Rinse but don't peel the sweet potatoes, and prick them a few times with a fork. Roast in a baking pan until tender, 45 to 60 minutes. Set aside for about 20 minutes to cool.

While the sweet potatoes cool, prepare the onions and kale. Warm a skillet over medium-low heat. Add the olive oil. Add the diced onion and sauté until soft and translucent, about 5 minutes. Add the kale and sauté for 1 or 2 minutes more, until the kale is wilted.

When cool enough to handle, slice the sweet potatoes in half lengthwise, carefully hollow each half with a spoon, and place the cooked flesh in a large mixing bowl. Add the onion and kale mixture, yogurt, Parmesan, thyme, and salt, and mix thoroughly to combine.

Using a spoon, carefully place a quarter of the filling into each sweet potato skin. Top the potatoes with the crumbled feta and return to the roasting pan.

Bake for another 15 to 20 minutes, until the cheese is golden and the sweet potatoes are thoroughly warmed. Allow to cool for 5 minutes, then serve.

SERVES 4

SWEET POTATO *and* THREE-BEAN CHILI

½ cup each of three dried bean varieties, such as snowcap, scarlet runner, and cranberry beans

2 large yellow onions, one halved, one diced

3 large cloves garlic, one halved, remaining minced

1 dried bay leaf

1 tablespoon extra-virgin olive oil

1 medium sweet potato (about 9 ounces), cut into small dice

1 to 2 teaspoons chipotle chile powder

1 tablespoon ancho chile powder

1 teaspoon ground cumin

1 (28-ounce) can crushed tomatoes (preferably fire-roasted)

2 teaspoons fine sea salt

1 teaspoon dried oregano

Monterey Jack cheese, coarsely grated, for serving

Fresh cilantro, for serving

Plain Greek yogurt, for serving

There is a cult around heirloom beans. I didn't get it at first. And then I tasted snowcap beans for the first time, and I understood. They have a creaminess about them that is luscious. They've become my favorite bean for chili. Using dried heirloom beans adds a lot of depth and texture to your bowl of chili, especially when it's vegetarian. Your bean choices in a chili are wide open: in addition to heirloom beans, you can use meaty Christmas lima beans, or petite black-eyed peas, or classic kidney or pinto beans. The versatile sweet potato adds a little sweetness without adding refined sugar. It's a hearty, filling bowl of smoky-sweet savory goodness. Note: You can use 4 cups of well-drained canned beans to save time soaking, and substitute chicken or vegetable broth for the bean water, if you like. *See photo, page 171.*

In a large bowl, soak the beans overnight in enough water to cover by about 2 inches. This will yield about 4 cups of beans after soaking.

Drain and rinse the beans. Add the beans to a large pot with enough water to cover by about 1 inch, along with the halved onion, halved garlic clove, and bay leaf. Cover and bring to a boil. Reduce the heat to low and simmer until the beans are cooked through but firm, about 45 to 60 minutes. Drain the beans, reserving 2 cups of the cooking liquid. Discard the onion, garlic, and bay leaf.

In a large heavy pot, heat the oil over medium-low heat, add the diced onion and minced garlic, and sauté until the onion is translucent, about 5 minutes, stirring regularly. Add the diced sweet potatoes and cook, stirring, for about 5 minutes more, until the sweet potatoes just begin to soften at the edges. Next, add the chipotle and ancho chile powders and the cumin and stir until fragrant, about

1 minute more. Add the beans, tomatoes, salt, oregano, and 1 cup of the reserved bean water to the pot. Cover and bring to a boil, then reduce the heat to low and simmer, stirring occasionally, until the sweet potatoes are cooked through, about 60 to 90 minutes. Remove from the heat. Allow to cool for about 15 minutes before serving, or cool to room temperature and then store in the fridge for up to 5 days. The flavors of the chili will improve if left to sit overnight.

To serve, reheat if necessary. Ladle into bowls and top with the cheese and fresh cilantro. Add a dollop of Greek yogurt for some creaminess, if desired.

SERVES 4 TO 6

ROOT VEGETABLE GRATIN

There is little that is more comforting than softly roasted root vegetables tucked beneath warm, melted cheese. This is an easy way to experiment with less familiar root vegetables, such as kohlrabi, turnips, or rutabagas. It's also a good opportunity to mix up the sweet and the savory—a blend of sweet potatoes or beets with the solid starchiness of a sturdy potato works really well here.

Preheat the oven to 375°F. Grease a 2½ quart oval baking dish with butter.

Using a mandoline or a large, sharp knife, slice the root vegetables into rounds about ¼ inch thick.

Combine the Gruyère and Pecorino cheeses in a small bowl.

Layer the root vegetables in the prepared baking dish, alternating different varieties. When the dish is about half full, lightly salt and pepper the vegetables, then sprinkle evenly with 1 cup of the combined cheeses and 1 teaspoon of the thyme. Add the remaining root vegetable slices. Slowly pour the broth over the dish. Add the remaining teaspoon of thyme and another pinch of salt.

Cover the dish with aluminum foil and bake for 40 minutes. Remove from the oven and carefully discard the foil. Sprinkle the remaining cheese on the vegetables, add a generous amount of pepper, and cook, uncovered, for another 10 to 15 minutes, until the cheese is golden and bubbly. Garnish with more thyme, if desired. Serve hot.

SERVES 8 TO 10

1 large russet potato (about 12 ounces)

1 small sweet potato (about 8 ounces)

1 small celery root (about 8 ounces), peeled

2 root vegetables, such as turnips, rutabagas, or beets (about ¾ pound total), peeled

1¼ cups grated Gruyère cheese

1¼ cups grated Pecorino cheese

Fine sea salt

Freshly ground black pepper

2 teaspoons chopped fresh thyme, plus more for garnish

¾ cup low-sodium vegetable broth

RED BEET RISOTTO

I must confess that I am not the biggest beet lover, but their dramatic magenta color calls out to me like a siren song. They're stunning things—but that deep earthy-sweet flavor is sometimes just a little much. When I cook with them, I like to tame that earthiness. I used sweet brown rice to incorporate a whole-grain element into traditionally starchy risotto, and it works well, adding a pleasing toothiness to the dish that you wouldn't find with Arborio rice, traditionally used in risotto. Everything else is a classic beet partner: the arugula, goat cheese, and Parmesan all balance that earthy flavor perfectly.

2 red beets

5 cups low-sodium vegetable broth

1 tablespoon unsalted butter

½ small red onion, diced

1 cup sweet brown rice (or use traditional Arborio rice)

2 ounces soft, fresh goat cheese

¼ cup freshly grated Parmesan cheese

¼ teaspoon fine sea salt

Freshly ground black pepper

1 cup loosely packed arugula, plus more for garnish

Preheat the oven to 400°F.

Pierce the beets with a fork, place them in a small baking dish, and cover with a snug-fitting lid or wrap the dish tightly with aluminum foil. Bake the beets for about 1 hour, until fork-tender. Remove from the oven and allow to cool. Once cool enough to handle, peel off the outer skins of the beets and cut into small dice, about ¼-inch square. You will have about 1 cup.

While the beets roast, make the risotto. Heat the broth in a small pot over low heat. Keep the broth warm but not quite simmering.

In a large pot over medium-low heat, melt the butter. Add the onion and sauté until translucent, 4 to 5 minutes. Add the rice and toast for about 5 minutes, until the rice begins to appear translucent around the edges. Add 1 cup of the broth and stir until nearly absorbed. Continue adding the broth in ½-cup increments, stirring regularly and adding the next ½ cup when most of the broth has been absorbed. When the rice is done, it will be creamy but still firm and chewy—more so than a traditional risotto made with Arborio rice. Remove from the heat.

Add the goat cheese, Parmesan, and salt and pepper to taste, and stir to combine. Add the diced beets and stir vigorously until the risotto absorbs the juices of the beets and turns a bright shade of pink. Add the arugula and mix again.

Serve warm, garnished with a bit more arugula and pepper.

SERVES 4

ROASTED BEETS
with CHIMICHURRI

7 to 8 small beets (select a variety, such as Chioggia, golden, and red beets)

CHIMICHURRI

¼ cup extra-virgin olive oil

2 tablespoons red wine vinegar

1 small shallot, thinly sliced

½ cup coarsely chopped fresh flat-leaf parsley

1 tablespoon finely chopped fresh oregano

½ teaspoon fine sea salt

¼ teaspoon dried red pepper flakes

Chimichurri is another great way to temper the intense, earthy flavor of beets. It's a wonderfully vibrant and lively sauce originally from Argentina and most frequently served as an accompaniment to steak. But chimichurri matches well with the big flavor of beets. To make this dish especially dynamic, go for a colorful selection of beet varieties, including the pink-and-white-striped Chioggias and lovely golden beets.

Preheat the oven to 400°F.

Pierce the beets with a fork, place them in a small baking dish, and cover with a snug-fitting lid or wrap the dish tightly with aluminum foil. Bake the beets for 45 to 60 minutes, until fork-tender. Remove from the oven and allow to cool.

While the beets roast, prepare the chimichurri. Combine the olive oil, wine vinegar, shallot, parsley, oregano, salt, and red pepper flakes in a small bowl. Whisk thoroughly and set aside.

Remove the skins from the beets. Slice the beets crosswise ½-inch thick. Carefully toss the beet slices with the chimichurri and serve immediately.

SERVES 4

VIBRANT FOOD

BRASSICAS

SHREDDED BRUSSELS SPROUTS *with* APPLES *and* MUSTARD SEEDS

Brussels sprouts, like cauliflower, rank high on my list of favored winter vegetables. It took a long time to come around to a slaw-like preparation, though, because I'm happy with them golden and caramelized in a hot pan with just salt and pepper. When my stepmom started making shredded brussels sprouts at Christmas, I was finally convinced. It's a hearty, simple side, and the mustard seeds offer a pleasing crunch.

½ cup raw pecans

16 ounces brussels sprouts

2 tablespoons apple cider vinegar

1 tablespoon plus 1 teaspoon honey

1 tablespoon brown mustard seeds

1 small shallot, minced

¾ teaspoon fine sea salt

Freshly ground black pepper

1 tablespoon extra-virgin olive oil

1 sweet-tart red apple, such as Braeburn or Pink Lady, cored and diced

Preheat the oven to 350°F

Arrange the pecans in a single layer on a baking sheet. Toast until golden brown and fragrant, about 8 to 10 minutes. Set aside to cool for about 5 minutes, then coarsely chop.

Thinly slice the brussels sprouts crosswise into ¼-inch rounds. Remove any of the woody stem that remains and, using your fingers, break up the sprouts into thin ribbons. Set aside.

To prepare the dressing, whisk together the cider vinegar, honey, mustard seeds, shallot, salt, and pepper to taste. Set aside.

In a large skillet over medium heat, warm the oil. Add the shredded brussels sprouts and sauté, stirring, until soft but still retaining some crunch, about 5 minutes. Add the dressing and cook for 1 to 2 minutes longer, stirring to combine. Remove from the heat to avoid wilting the sprouts. Toss the apples and pecans with the brussels sprouts. Serve immediately.

SERVES 4

ROASTED CAULIFLOWER
with OLIVES, CURRANTS,
and TAHINI DRESSING

1 large cauliflower (about
3 pounds), trimmed and cut
into florets

3 tablespoons extra-virgin olive oil

Fine sea salt

¼ cup currants

¼ cup coarsely chopped
kalamata olives

¼ cup coarsely chopped fresh
flat-leaf parsley

TAHINI DRESSING

¼ cup tahini

2 tablespoons freshly squeezed
lemon juice

1½ teaspoons extra-virgin olive oil

1 small clove garlic, minced

⅛ teaspoon fine sea salt

2 tablespoons water, plus
more as needed

There are certain vegetables for which I have an intense fondness, and
cauliflower is one of them. I could eat a head of caramelized cauliflower in
one sitting and still wish for more. It's the gentlest of the brassicas, I think.
There's something lovely happening here, between the earthy tanginess of the
tahini dressing, the sharp and salty umami of the olives, the little bursts of
sweetness from the currants, and the herbal brightness of the parsley.

Preheat the oven to 400°F.

Toss the cauliflower florets with the olive oil and a sprinkle of sea salt to taste.
Arrange the cauliflower florets in a single layer on a large rimmed baking
sheet. Roast for about 20 minutes, turning once, until the edges are brown and
caramelized.

While the cauliflower roasts, make the dressing. Whisk together the tahini,
lemon juice, olive oil, garlic, and salt until smooth and creamy. Add the water and
whisk until combined. The sauce will be thick. Add more water to thin it slightly
if you like. It will continue to thicken as it sits.

Toss the warm cauliflower with most of the dressing. Add the currants, olives,
and parsley and toss to combine. Taste and add more dressing or salt, if desired.

Serve warm or at room temperature.

SERVES 4

BABY KALE CAESAR SALAD

CROUTONS

2 cups torn 1-inch pieces
crusty bread

1 tablespoon extra-virgin olive oil

¼ teaspoon fine sea salt

CAESAR DRESSING

8 anchovies, rinsed

1 egg yolk

1 teaspoon Dijon mustard

5 tablespoons extra-virgin olive oil

2 tablespoons freshly squeezed
lemon juice

2 tablespoons red wine vinegar

2 garlic cloves, minced

8 cups loosely packed baby kale,
such as Red Russian

¼ cup freshly grated Parmesan
cheese

I love using tender young kale leaves in place of a Caesar's traditional romaine lettuce. Kale has a more robust flavor than romaine, which tames the intensity of the dressing. Baby kale leaves are ideal for their tenderness, but mature Red Russian kale will work just fine as well. (If you use mature kale leaves instead of baby kale, remove the stems, tear the leaves into bite-size pieces, and allow the dressed kale to sit for about 20 minutes before serving, to tenderize the leaves.) I went to great lengths to pull together a big, bold Caesar dressing inspired by some of my favorites in San Francisco: Zuni Cafe's famous Caesar and Slow Club's equally tangy version.

Preheat the oven to 400°F.

To make the croutons, toss the bread with the olive oil and salt on a sheet pan and spread to form an even layer. Bake for about 8 minutes, tossing halfway, until crisp and golden. Set aside to cool.

Make the anchovies into a paste by using the side of a sharp knife to smash the anchovies and then finely mince them, continuing until you have a coarse paste.

In a mixing bowl, whisk together the egg yolk, Dijon mustard, and minced anchovies. Slowly whisk in the olive oil in a thin, steady stream. Add the lemon juice, wine vinegar, and garlic. Whisk vigorously to emulsify.

Toss the baby kale leaves and the dressing with your hands to thoroughly coat the leaves.

Divide the dressed kale among four plates and sprinkle with the Parmesan and croutons. This salad is best served immediately.

SERVES 4

CURRIED WINTER SLAW

Cabbage is among the humblest of vegetables. I cannot shake its association with long, dreary winters and sparse meals composed of boiled meats and this challenging crucifer. But there's much to be made of that deep purple hue—it's gorgeous as the foundation for a big winter slaw. Using garam masala, an Indian spice mixture used in many Indian dishes, adds a welcome warming note to this slaw. The apples, almonds, and cranberries add texture, color, and sweetness to the cabbage base. If one must have a salad in the winter, this is a hearty choice.

Preheat the oven to 325°F.

In a small mixing bowl, whisk together the honey, garam masala, cinnamon, ginger, and salt to create a thick paste. Whisk in the lime juice and zest. Stir in the yogurt until the sauce is smooth.

Add the cabbage to a large serving bowl. Pour the dressing over the cabbage and gently toss together to coat evenly. Let it sit, covered and in the refrigerator, for 1 to 3 hours, until the flavors meld and mellow, mixing once or twice.

While the cabbage rests, toast the nuts. Spread the almonds in a single layer on a baking sheet and toast in the oven, stirring occasionally, for about 10 minutes, until fragrant and golden. Coarsely chop the nuts and set aside.

Add the toasted almonds, apples, and cranberries to the cabbage mix and combine thoroughly.

Serve cold or at room temperature.

SERVES 8

2 tablespoons honey

1½ teaspoons garam masala (choose a blend with no salt added)

¼ teaspoon ground cinnamon

¼ teaspoon ground ginger

1 teaspoon fine sea salt

Zest and juice of 1 lime

¾ cup plain whole milk Greek yogurt

1 medium red cabbage (about 1½ pounds), quartered, cored, and very thinly sliced

1 cup whole raw almonds

2 large sweet-tart red apples, such as Pink Lady, cored and thinly sliced

1 cup dried cranberries

VIBRANT FOOD

Dungeness
CRAB

CRAB CAKES *with* POACHED EGGS

Crab cakes paired with a runny poached egg are among my favorite fancy weekend breakfasts. I prefer a crab cake that is heavy on the crab and light on everything else, which is a delicate balancing act—too little egg or bread crumbs, and your cakes won't stay together; too much, and they don't taste like crab. This version aims to land in the sweet spot. It's tucked away here in the winter section because that's when our West Coast Dungeness crab peaks. Most any kind of lump crab meat will do.

To make the crab cakes, whisk the egg in a mixing bowl and set aside. In a large mixing bowl, combine the yogurt, parsley, chives, mustard, lemon juice, paprika, cayenne pepper, and black pepper and mix. Add the crab and egg carefully and mix until just combined to preserve the texture of the crab. Add the bread crumbs and lightly mix again. Season with a generous pinch of salt. Divide into eight portions and shape into cakes about 1 inch thick. Chill for 1 hour.

Preheat the oven to 200°F. Remove the crab cakes from the fridge. Warm a large skillet over medium heat and add 1 tablespoon of the olive oil. Working in batches, add the crab cakes to the hot skillet, three or four at a time, being careful not to crowd them. Pan-fry until golden brown at the edges, 3 to 4 minutes. Flip and repeat. Transfer to a plate and keep warm in the oven. Heat the remaining 1 tablespoon of olive oil and repeat with the second batch. Keep the crab cakes warm in the oven until the eggs are ready.

To make the poached eggs, fill a wide, shallow pan with about 2 inches of water and bring to a very gentle, barely bubbling simmer. Add a splash of vinegar. Crack each egg into a small ramekin. Use tongs to lower the ramekin into the water, allowing water to fill the cup and surround the egg for about 15 seconds. Gently pour the egg out of the ramekin and repeat for the remaining eggs. Poach for 3 to 4 minutes, until the white are set. Remove the eggs with a slotted spoon and set aside on a paper towel–lined plate.

To serve, set two crab cakes on each plate and top with one poached egg. Garnish with fresh parsley and paprika. Serve immediately.

SERVES 4

CRAB CAKES

1 egg

2 tablespoons plain Greek yogurt

2 tablespoons chopped fresh flat-leaf parsley, plus more for garnish

2 tablespoons finely minced fresh chives

1 tablespoon Dijon mustard

1 tablespoon freshly squeezed lemon juice

¼ teaspoon sweet paprika, plus more for garnish

⅛ teaspoon cayenne pepper

Freshly ground black pepper

16 ounces good-quality lump crabmeat

¼ cup bread crumbs

Fine sea salt

2 tablespoons extra-virgin olive oil

4 eggs

White vinegar

COCONUT SEAFOOD CHOWDER

1 tablespoon extra-virgin olive oil

4 medium shallots, sliced crosswise

2-inch knob fresh ginger, sliced into coins

1 stalk lemongrass, tough outer stalk removed, sliced into 2-inch pieces

4 cups low-sodium vegetable broth

1 (15-ounce) can full-fat coconut milk

3 tablespoons green curry paste

3 tablespoons fish sauce

12 ounces baby potatoes, such as marble potatoes, halved

1 Dungeness crab (about 2 pounds), cracked and cleaned

16 ounces fresh mussels, scrubbed

12 ounces firm white fish, such as Pacific cod, cut into 1½-inch pieces

12 to 16 sprigs cilantro, leaves plucked from stems

3 to 4 green onions, white and pale green parts only, thinly sliced

2 limes, sliced into wedges

Among the most comforting of foods on a gray winter evening is a steaming bowl of something stewy to brace against the cold. I'm enamored with the warmth and vibrancy that green curry paste, ginger, and lemongrass add to chowder. This is a marriage of two classics: a Thai-style curry and a New England seafood chowder. Use colorful baby marble potatoes for variety, if you can find them.

Heat the oil in a large stockpot over medium-low heat. Add the shallots and sauté until soft, 2 to 3 minutes. Add the ginger and lemongrass and sauté until fragrant, about 3 minutes.

Add the broth, coconut milk, curry paste, and fish sauce and mix thoroughly to combine. You may have to break up the curry paste with the back of a spoon. Cover, increase heat to high, and bring to a boil. Decrease the heat to medium-low; add the potatoes and cover. Cook for 5 minutes. Add the crab, mussels, and fish, and cover again. Cook until the mussels have opened, 6 to 8 minutes. Remove and discard any mussels that haven't opened.

Transfer the chowder from the heat and discard the ginger and lemongrass. Ladle into serving bowls. Garnish with the cilantro leaves and green onions, and serve with lime wedges on the side.

SERVES 6 TO 8

CITRUS

CORNMEAL PANCAKES
with KUMQUAT SYRUP

Kumquats are a lovely little citrus fruit whose skins are sweet and flesh bitter. Tamed with sugar, their sweet and tart qualities meld into a zesty syrup that is reminiscent of marmalade. The kumquats and their syrup are delicious not only with pancakes but also on yogurt or oatmeal.

To prepare the syrup, slice the kumquats crosswise about ⅛-inch thick, discarding the ends and seeds as you go.

Heat the water and sugar over medium heat in a small covered pot. When the sugar dissolves, add the kumquats and turn the heat to low. Simmer, uncovered, until the kumquats are soft but not falling apart, 10 to 15 minutes. Turn off the heat and remove the kumquats from the syrup.

Return the syrup to the stove and increase the heat to high. Boil the syrup to reduce it by half, about 10 minutes. Remove from the heat and combine the syrup with the kumquats. Set aside.

To make the pancakes, in a large mixing bowl, combine the flour, cornmeal, sugar, baking powder, baking soda, cardamom, and salt.

In a separate bowl, whisk together the buttermilk, eggs, olive oil, and orange zest. Pour the wet mix into the dry and stir until just combined.

Heat a 10-inch skillet over medium heat. When the skillet is hot, add ½ tablespoon of the butter and melt. Measure a scant ¼ cup of the pancake batter into the pan for each pancake, making about 3 pancakes per batch. Cook without disturbing until the edges of the pancakes begin to brown and they lift easily from the pan, about 3 minutes. Flip once and cook for about 2 more minutes. Repeat with the remaining batter, adding more butter to the pan for each batch. Adjust the heat as necessary so that the pancakes cook consistently.

Ladle the kumquats and their syrup over the pancakes just before serving.

SERVES 4 TO 6

KUMQUAT SYRUP

8 ounces kumquats, rinsed

1 cup water

½ cup natural cane sugar

CORNMEAL PANCAKES

1½ cups all-purpose flour (or use all-purpose gluten-free flour)

½ cup coarse cornmeal

3 tablespoons natural cane sugar

2 teaspoons baking powder

1 teaspoon baking soda

1 teaspoon ground cardamom

½ teaspoon fine sea salt

2 cups buttermilk

2 eggs, lightly beaten

2 tablespoons extra-virgin olive oil

Zest of 1 orange

2 tablespoons unsalted butter, plus more if needed

KIWI GRAPEFRUIT PARFAIT
with ROSE WATER

3 kiwis, peeled

2 grapefruits, such as Ruby Red, Rio Red, or Cocktail

3 tablespoons honey

1 tablespoon rose water

¼ teaspoon ground cardamom

1 cup plain Greek yogurt

1 cup granola

2 tablespoons toasted coconut flakes

Parfait is the kind of weekend brunch treat that feels fancy but is really simple to prepare. You alternate layers of yogurt, fruit, and granola and repeat. Different types of grapefruit offer so much variety in shades of pink, orange, and yellow, and the bright interplay of grapefruit shades with the soft green of the kiwi is lovely at the brunch table.

First, quarter the kiwis lengthwise. Slice each quarter crosswise into four pieces. Each kiwi will yield sixteen small wedges. Place in a mixing bowl.

Supreme the grapefruits. To do this, use a sharp paring knife to slice the top and bottom from the grapefruit. Carefully slice away the peel, working in segments around the outside of the fruit. Make sure to slice away as much of the white pith as possible.

Next, carefully slice on either side of the skin that separates the segments of fruit, removing just the sweet flesh of the grapefruit while leaving behind any bitter pith or skin. Slice each segment into thirds. Add them to the bowl with the kiwi wedges.

Add the honey, rose water, and cardamom to the fruit, stirring carefully with a spoon. The grapefruit may break apart a little, but this is fine.

Spoon ¼ cup of the yogurt into an 8- to 10-ounce dessert glass or wide-mouth jar. Follow with a quarter of the fruit mixture. Next, add ¼ cup of granola. Repeat, adding another ¼ cup of yogurt, a quarter of the fruit mixture, and ¼ cup granola. Top with half of the coconut flakes. Repeat with the second glass.

Serve immediately—the granola will get soggy if left to sit.

SERVES 2

VIBRANT FOOD

BLACK BEAN PATTIES *with* AVOCADO CITRUS SALSA

PATTIES

1 (15-ounce) can black beans, rinsed and thoroughly drained

½ cup cooked and cooled brown rice

¼ cup diced red onion

¼ cup chopped raw shelled pumpkin seeds

¼ cup bread crumbs

¼ cup crumbled feta cheese

1 egg, lightly beaten

2 tablespoons chopped fresh flat-leaf parsley

½ teaspoon chipotle chile powder

½ teaspoon ground cumin

½ teaspoon sweet paprika

½ teaspoon fine sea salt

2 tablespoons extra-virgin olive oil, plus more as needed

AVOCADO CITRUS SALSA

1 grapefruit

2 tangerines (or use clementines or mandarins)

1 avocado, diced

¼ cup chopped fresh cilantro

¼ small red onion, diced

½ jalapeño, seeded and finely minced

Juice of 1 lime

½ teaspoon fine sea salt

Black bean burgers really didn't stand out for me until I found myself at a small lodge in the southern Oregon wilderness with a cozy, unassuming café on the property. It was the kind of place where you might expect watery coffee and rubbery eggs. The thing is, they had a remarkable black bean burger. The surprise of this savory pile of spicy goodness on their menu absolutely made my day—and convinced me to try making my own version of this humble patty. I learned the hard way that using a food processor causes a veggie burger to lose much of its texture, which makes for a less interesting burger, so I prefer to mix them by hand. These burgers have a little kick, but the bright, cooling flavors of the citrus and avocado salsa temper them. Note that you'll likely have to make more than ½ cup of brown rice at a time. (I've found that 1 cup dry brown rice in 2 cups water works well, boiled then simmered for about 40 minutes—you can store the extra in the fridge for up to 5 days or the freezer for up to a month.) *See photo, page 203.*

To make the patties, combine the beans, rice, onion, pumpkin seeds, bread crumbs, feta cheese, egg, parsley, chipotle powder, cumin, paprika, and salt in a bowl. Use your hands to mix thoroughly. The mixture should be textured but well combined, with both whole and mashed beans. Divide the mixture into eight small patties, about 1 inch thick. Place the patties on a small baking sheet and chill for at least 30 minutes.

While the patties chill, make the salsa. Supreme the grapefruit. To do so, use a very sharp paring knife to slice the top and bottom from the grapefruit. Carefully slice away the peel, working in segments around the outside of the fruit. Make sure to slice away as much of the white pith as possible. Next, carefully slice on either side of the skin that separates the segments of fruit, removing just the sweet flesh of the grapefruit while leaving behind any bitter pith or skin. Repeat with the tangerines. Slice the grapefruit segments in half.

Combine the grapefruit and tangerines in a mixing bowl. Gently toss in the avocado, cilantro, red onion, jalapeño, lime juice, and salt and stir to combine. Set aside.

To cook the patties, heat a large skillet over medium heat. Add 1 tablespoon of the olive oil. Remove the patties from the fridge. Working in batches, add four patties to the pan at a time, gently pressing each with a spatula. Cook the patties, without disturbing, until a deep brown crust has formed on the bottom, about 5 minutes. Flip and cook for another 4 minutes. Transfer to a paper towel–lined plate and repeat with the remaining patties.

To serve, place two patties on each plate and top each with a generous dollop of the avocado citrus salsa.

SERVES 4

YOGURT PAPRIKA CHICKEN *with* LEMON

This marinade was inspired by tandoori chicken—among my favorite ways to eat chicken because it so masterfully preserves moisture and makes for the most succulent dark meat. The bold red essence of paprika, which comes from dried peppers, is a knockout. Squeezing a little of the juice of the roasted lemon on the chicken right before eating adds a lovely hit of acid.

¾ cup plain Greek yogurt

1 tablespoon minced fresh ginger

1 tablespoon sweet paprika

1 teaspoon ground cumin

2 large garlic cloves, minced

2 tablespoons freshly squeezed lemon juice

1 teaspoon fine sea salt

2 pounds chicken thighs and drumsticks

2 lemons, halved

Chopped fresh cilantro, for garnish

In a large mixing bowl, combine the yogurt, ginger, paprika, cumin, garlic, lemon juice, and salt. Toss the chicken into the marinade, generously coating all sides of the meat. Cover and refrigerate for 1 hour.

Preheat the oven to 400°F.

Remove the chicken from the fridge and arrange in a single layer on a roasting pan. Nestle the lemon halves among the pieces of chicken. Roast for about 30 minutes, until the chicken registers 165°F on an instant-read thermometer.

Finish the chicken 6 inches under the broiler for 3 to 5 minutes, until the chicken is just beginning to blacken in places. Garnish with a generous sprinkle of chopped cilantro. Serve with the roasted lemons on the side to squeeze over the chicken.

SERVES 4

SPARKLING POMEGRANATE PUNCH

GINGER SIMPLE SYRUP

½ cup coarsely chopped fresh ginger

½ cup natural cane sugar

½ cup water

PUNCH

1 (750 ml) bottle dry, chilled sparkling wine

½ navel orange, juiced

½ lemon, juiced

½ clementine or tangerine, juiced

4 ounces (½ cup) gin, chilled

½ cup pomegranate seeds

Citrus slices for garnish, such as navel oranges, Cara Cara oranges, tangerine, lemons, or limes

Ice, for serving

My birthday is at the start of December, and between that, Christmas, and New Year's, most of the month feels like one big, extended celebration. I love to throw a party somewhere in the middle of the month, and a celebratory punch is essential. This version was inspired by a festive punch featured on the now-defunct food website Gilt Taste. Citrus is perfect here, not only for its color but also the sweet acid brightness it brings to the drink. It's wise to double this if making it for a large get-together.

To make the simple syrup, combine the ginger, sugar, and water in a small saucepan. Bring to a simmer and stir until the sugar dissolves. Simmer for 30 minutes, stirring occasionally. Remove from the heat and allow to cool completely. Strain out the ginger and discard. Store the simple syrup in the refrigerator until needed.

To make the punch, combine the sparkling wine, orange juice, lemon juice, clementine juice, gin, and ginger syrup in a punch bowl. Garnish with the pomegranate seeds and citrus slices. Serve over ice.

SERVES 4 TO 6